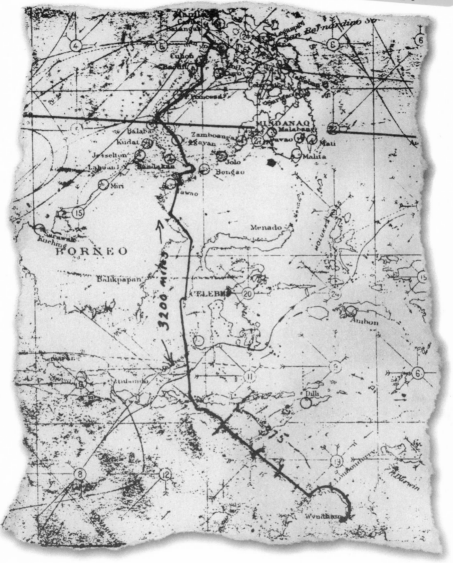

A map marked after the escape, detailing the route
from the Philippines (top) to Australia.

THE WAR
JOURNAL
OF MAJOR DAMON "ROCKY" GAUSE

THE WAR JOURNAL

OF MAJOR DAMON "ROCKY" GAUSE

MAJOR DAMON "ROCKY" GAUSE

with an Introduction by Damon L. Gause

HYPERION

New York

This book is dedicated to all American defenders of freedom, both the living and the deceased.

FOREWORD

ROCKY GAUSE WAS AN ORDINARY MAN CAUGHT up in extraordinary times. He responded with such courage, grace, determination, strength, willpower, and patriotism to inspire us all. There was no risk he would not take, whether fighting against the Japanese or the Germans. He died testing a P-47's dive capability just before D-Day, but he lives today thanks to his accomplishments and recording of them.

I recommend this book without stint or hesitation to everyone who has read *Endurance, The Perfect Storm, Into Thin Air, The Greatest Generation, Undaunted Courage,* or the other accounts of great, inspiring, almost unbelievable—except that they really happened—adventures. I'd further recommend it to anyone who thinks the Japanese behavior in World War II has been maligned.

This magnificent book fills one with pride just for being a human being. It makes us all wonder, Could I have done that? And glad beyond measure that Major Damon Gause did it—and that he was on our side.

—Stephen E. Ambrose

INTRODUCTION

THE STORY YOU ARE ABOUT TO READ is a remarkable first-person account by an American soldier, Major Damon "Rocky" Gause. It is Major Gause's memoir of his capture by the Japanese during the outbreak of World War II in the Philippine Islands, his escape from the Bataan death march, and his miraculous 3,200-mile voyage to Australia—and freedom—in a twenty-foot wooden fishing boat.

An Army Air Corps dive-bomber pilot with the 27th Bombardment Group, then-Lieutenant Gause was stationed in Manila during December of 1941. There he witnessed the siege and eventual fall of the Philippines into Japanese hands, the retreat of the American army to the jungle-infested Bataan Peninsula, and the flight of the American Forces' Far East commander, General Douglas MacArthur, to the safety of Australia. Gause was one of 70,000 estimated American and Filipino soldiers captured by the Japanese and destined to walk what would later go down in history as the infamous Bataan Death March—a grueling sixty-four-mile forced march to prisoner-holding pens. Although the exact figures will never be known, approximately 10,000 Filipino and American servicemen died from hunger, thirst, disease, and the brutality of the enemy captors along the death march route.

Not only did Gause escape the Bataan Death March in April of 1942, he later swam three miles through shark-infested waters to the rock-island fortress of Corregidor to join the last American troops still fighting the Japanese. When Corregidor fell in May, Gause eluded capture by island-hopping for three months, staying one step ahead of enemy patrols bent on his capture. On the island of Mindoro, Gause met a fellow American escapee, Captain William Lloyd Osborne, and together they embarked upon a harrowing voyage across the enemy-held Pacific Ocean. For fifty-two days, they dodged scores of enemy patrols, weathered tropical storms, ran aground on uncharted coral reefs, made countless makeshift repairs, landed briefly at the world's largest leper colony, lived on an ever-dwindling supply of fish, coconuts, bananas, rice, and rainwater, and barely survived a strafing from a Japanese fighter plane before finally reaching Wyndham on the northwest coast of Australia.

Just ten days after reaching Australia, Gause and Osborne were personally awarded the Distinguished Service Cross by General MacArthur for "extraordinary heroism in action." Stories and pictures about their heroics appeared in newspapers and magazines across the country— The *New York Daily Mirror* ran a 22-part interview with Captain Gause and Captain Osborne. Their courage captured the imagination of people around the world.

From the battered ship's log and the handmade diary he kept throughout the journey, Gause worked during the months following his return to safety to craft an account of his escape. After completing the manuscript, he paid a sergeant to type it for him. An excerpt ran in the *New York Times Magazine* (the editors headlined it "An epic tale of hopeless heroism and daring flight") announcing that it would be published in the near future by Macmillan under the title "By the Grace of God . . . and the Filipinos." But there were problems such as obtaining the necessary permission from the War Department and so the book was never published. This is the story you now hold in your hands, the story in his own words of one American hero—my father.

MY FATHER RETURNED HOME to a hero's welcome in November of 1942 and was reunited with the young bride he had married just two weeks prior to going overseas. He remained home in the States for thirteen months, during which time I was conceived and born. When I was two days old, my father visited me in the hospital for a few scant hours before returning overseas, this time to the European theater of operations. The date was December 9, 1943, and it was destined to be the only time he and I were ever together.

On March 3, 1944, an associate editor at Macmillan wrote to my mother asking her to let my father know that they couldn't reconsider publication—that several books about subsequent escapes were coming out and that they still didn't know how to obtain permission from the War Department for the release of potentially sensitive materials.

Just seven days later, on March 10, 1944, my mother received a telegram from the War Department informing her that the P-47 my father was flying had crashed near London, England, and that my father had been killed. Several weeks later, an army footlocker arrived on her doorstep. Inside were my father's personal belongings from his two World War II tours of duty overseas. Items from his first tour included:

- the bayonet he used to kill a Japanese prison guard
- an American flag that flew over Corregidor
- the handheld compass used to navigate the voyage
- the chart used to plot the course of the voyage
- the ship's log
- my father's typescript based on the ship's log and his diary, which is printed in its entirety in the book you now hold

My mother placed other mementos inside the footlocker—the tattered clothing my father had worn during the historic voyage and nearly fifty photographs taken during the voyage, photographs captured with a camera and eight rolls of film he obtained from an American missionary on a remote island in midjourney. But the most precious item—and the item dearest to my mother's heart—was the handmade diary my father constructed right before the voyage by placing a stack of hand-cut paper between two pieces of cardboard and binding everything together with a length of copper wire.

My mother suddenly found herself a widow at the age of twenty-two—and this was all that remained of her beloved husband. She would never be able to place flowers upon her dead husband's grave, so this would serve as his tomb. Determined to preserve the contents of the foot-locker, my mother stored it inside a closet in a back bed-room of her home and there it has remained all these years, unveiled to family members from time to time, but off-limits to the general public.

During the years that followed the end of World War II, my mother received several overtures from publishers who wanted to publish my father's story, but found herself torn each time. She was proud of my father and wanted the world to learn about his accomplishments, but she had tried to move on with her life, and eventually remarried. She was hesitant about allowing the ghost of her dead hus-band to intrude into her relationship with her new hus-band, Jefferson, Georgia, businessman Vernon Carter, himself a World War II veteran who had survived the bombing of Pearl Harbor. She was equally hesitant about allowing the ghost of my dead father to intrude into my relationship with my new stepfather.

Even after she saw the new relationships grow into a harmonious homelife, she remained concerned about me. To her, the contents of the footlocker represented my fa-ther's legacy to his only child. She decided to wait, to allow me the opportunity to make my own decision about if and when my father's story would be published.

For me, the decision was a long time coming.

I can remember being barely old enough to walk when General Jonathan M. "Skinny" Wainwright, my father's commanding officer on Corregidor, came to my home-town for a short visit. I can also remember being a young-ster and meeting General George C. Marshall—the army chief of staff who later became the only person to serve as both secretary of defense and secretary of state, and the author of the Marshall Plan. I can still picture General Marshall sitting in his rocker with a blanket wrapped around his knees, beckoning me closer, taking me by the hand, and telling me, "Never let the memory of your father lay forgotten. He could never say die, and we'll always need men like him."

I was well into my adult years before I finally grasped the meaning of General Marshall's words and realized that it was up to me, my father's only child, to keep his memory and accomplishments alive. It took longer still for me to realize how important it was for my mother to see my father's deeds immortalized in print. Only last year did it finally dawn on me that she had advanced into her late seventies and wasn't going to live forever. If my mother was going to see my father's story published, it was now or never.

THERE IS NO WAY TO COUNT the number of times my mother dragged the old footlocker out of the closet, opened it, and told me stories about what was inside. Nor can I count the number of times over the years that I've read and reread my father's exploits.

Every summer while I was growing up, I stayed with my paternal grandparents, listened to hundreds of stories and recollections about my father, and gained valuable insight about what it was in his upbringing and physical makeup that instilled in him the taste for adventure, the daring, the skill, and the will to survive the hell of war. My grand-

mother, grandfather, aunts, and uncles all described someone who sounded to me like Huckleberry Finn—someone
who preferred the outdoors to the indoors, learned to swim
at the age of six, and was adventurous and rambunctious,
someone who disappeared into the swamps for weekends
at a time as a teenager and lived off the land by hunting,
fishing, and trapping—a daredevil who believed he could
do anything he set out to do.

Over the years I have spoken to nearly every resident in
my father's hometown of Jefferson, Georgia, population
2,000—many of them former friends, neighbors, and
classmates of his. They described someone who found the
classroom confining and studying a bore, yet combined
basic intelligence with good common sense to do just well
enough to please his parents. They spoke of a warm, caring
young man, someone with a good sense of humor, quick
to accept a challenge, someone who championed the cause
of the underdog. These qualities made him well-liked and
well-respected by his peers, and contributed to the char-
ismatic personality that drew people to him. My grandmother once told me, "Damon, had your father survived
the war, I believe he would have become the governor of
Georgia one day."

Despite my success in accumulating information about
my father, two gaps remained. I didn't know anything
about the time from when my father embarked for the
Philippines in November of 1941 until his story begins on
New Year's Eve 1941—only two months, but an extremely
critical period—nor did I know anything about what happened after he arrived in Europe on his second World War
II tour of duty.

Hoping to bridge those gaps, I became a World War II buff, accumulated an extensive library that includes many books long since out of print, and began speaking to groups of veterans. After a speech a few years back, I met Bert Schwarz—a close friend of my father's, a former member of one of my father's outfits, the 27th Bombardment Group, and a survivor of the Bataan death march. As soon as he learned of my interest in finding veterans who served with my father, he put me in contact with former members of the 27th, including the son of Clay Conner. Clay Conner was a close friend of my father, a fellow officer, and someone who played a significant role in my father's story. Conner's son was able to provide me with invaluable information I could not have obtained anywhere else. I also contacted General James Hill, a former Air Force chief of staff who served with my father when they were both majors with the 365th Fighter Group in England, and he told me about the period leading up to my father's death.

Today, I travel throughout the South speaking to groups of veterans such as the American Legion, the Veterans of Foreign Wars, the National Chapter of the Defenders of Bataan and Corregidor, and at annual reunions of the 27th Bombardment Group. My speeches are patriotic, pro-American, and pro-Filipino and come from the heart, without notes, and often culminate in standing ovations. Afterward, I talk to hundreds of old soldiers, many of them with tears in their eyes, and listen to tales of *their* exploits. It is also for them—the members of my father's generation who sacrificed so much in the name of freedom, for their country, for their families, every one of them a hero—that this book is now being published.

• • •

THE WAR JOURNAL OF MAJOR DAMON "ROCKY" GAUSE begins in the Empire Room of the Manila Hotel on New Year's Eve of 1941, twenty-three days after the bombing of Pearl Harbor, but my father didn't explain the circumstances and events that placed him there. To fill in the missing details, I will now take you back in time and provide information that I believe is essential to your understanding of the journal:

My father stood five feet, five-and-a-half inches tall and weighed 165 pounds. Photographs show him to be fairly stocky and, as a result of spending so much time outdoors, his face was deeply tanned year-round.

After graduating from Martin Institute high school in Jefferson, my father attended the University of Georgia in Athens, but found the college classroom as uninspiring as the high school classroom. More to his liking was a small airfield outside of Athens called Ben T. Epps Field. Already in love with driving automobiles and driving them fast, he looked at flying as a natural extension of his passion for speed, began taking flying lessons at Epps Field, and became a pilot.

During that same period he also discovered an old wooden inn—Rambler's Inn—outside of Jefferson where prizefights were held on Friday and Saturday nights. Having found something else that appealed to his basic instincts, he began a training program of running to and from school, shadowboxing while he ran, and soon became a boxer. Between flying, boxing, and a thirst for adventure, college didn't stand a chance.

My father dropped out of college after one year to enlist in the Coast Guard and served a tour of duty as a radioman on the Coast Guard cutter *Argo*. After being honorably discharged, he enlisted in the Army Corps and was posted to the Panama Canal Zone, where, in addition to his duties as a radioman and gunner, he was also a news correspondent for Press Wireless. After being honorably discharged a second time, he took a job with the Texaco oil company and was soon bound for Barranquilla, Colombia, and worked in South America until 1939, when his fascination with airplanes led him to the Civil Aeronautics Administration back home in Georgia. First, he worked at a small airfield in Alma, then moved to Candler Field outside of Atlanta, a small airport, which would evolve into today's Hartsfield International Airport. In addition to his official duties with the Civil Aeronautics Administration, he logged hundreds of hours in the air as a pilot.

That was when my mother, Ruth Evans, then age nineteen, entered his life.

One of my father's sisters had graduated from high school in Jefferson with my mother, and they remained good friends. Being six years my father's junior, my mother never knew him during her school days. They met when he came home to visit and my aunt introduced them. My mother had grown up on a small farm, the youngest of four sisters, and had never ventured outside of Jackson County, where she was born and raised. When my father asked her to go to a fancy hotel in Atlanta for dinner, she jumped at the chance. But their courtship was destined to run anything but smoothly.

It was the beginning of 1941 and most of the world was

already embroiled in World War II. Although the United States had not yet joined the fight, it seemed inevitable to my father and he decided to enlist once again. This time he qualified for the U.S. Army Air Corps cadet school and was sent to Randolph Field in Texas for flight training, then on to Kelly Field, also in Texas, for advanced flight training. When he was ready to receive his wings, he sent Ruth an invitation to attend the graduation ceremony.

By then she had completed a business course and was working as a secretary for a local electrical cooperative company. Unable to arrange sufficient time off from work to travel to Texas, she declined the invitation. That was when fate intervened on their behalf.

After earning his wings, my father was assigned to the 27th Bombardment Group and stationed at Hunter Field in Savannah, Georgia, less than three hundred miles from Jefferson, enabling my mother and father to resume their courtship. She sometimes went to Savannah and he sometimes came home, but just as their romance was beginning to bloom, another interruption came long.

In September of 1941, the 27th Bombardment Group was deployed for maneuvers to Lake Charles, Louisiana. With thousands of soldiers playing war games in the bayous, this was the biggest maneuver ever conducted by the U.S. Army and a lesson in jungle warfare designed to prepare them for what loomed ahead. It was a foreign experience for most of the soldiers, and dangerous—two deaths resulted from the bites of coral snakes—but it was exactly what my father had been doing all his life in the name of fun, and he excelled at it.

Maneuvers ended at the beginning of October and the

27th Bombardment Group returned to Savannah. As a member of the Communications group, my father was one of the first to learn that classified orders had been issued to send the 27th overseas to the Philippine Islands—code name: Operation Plum. Departure was slated for November 7—just one month hence.

By then my father had become hopelessly infatuated with my mother. The way he saw it, she was the woman with whom he wanted to spend the rest of his life. Acting with a sense of urgency and unbeknownst to her, he bought two rings with both of their names inscribed, then proposed. This did catch my mother by surprise and she was hesitant—mostly because of the difference in their ages—but he wooed her, won her over, and she accepted.

In keeping with the custom in the South back then, my father went to my mother's parents and asked for her hand in marriage. Her mother readily gave her consent, but her father was not as agreeable. He was a country farmer who believed that a man should own a piece of land with a house on it before taking on the responsibility of marriage. Army life and moving around the country sounded strange to him, so he asked them to wait.

This was not what my parents wanted to hear. They were planning to get married and planning to have my mother join him in the Philippines as soon as possible. On October 11, my mother and father eloped and got married. The honeymoon ended soon.

Two weeks after the wedding, my father went by train to San Francisco, California, and there boarded the S.S. *President Coolidge*, a former luxury liner pressed into military service, bound for the Philippines. With the navy cruiser U.S.S. *Louisville* acting as escort, the convoy proceeded under wartime blackout precautions—all portholes were covered with curtains after nightfall and there was no smoking on deck. With no official duties to perform at sea, my father passed the time by reading, shooting dice, and playing cards with two men he had befriended since first arriving at Fort Hunter in Savannah—Lieutenant Clay Conner and Lieutenant Leroy Cowert.

Halfway to the Philippines, the *President Coolidge* docked in Pearl Harbor to refuel and to take on supplies. While in port, my father toured the island of Oahu with his two buddies, visiting Waikiki Beach, Diamond Head, and as many tourist attractions as time allowed. Then it was back to sea.

On November 27, the *President Coolidge* sailed into Manila, and the soldiers of the 27th were loaded into trucks and whisked through the city. They were supposed to be quartered at Fort Stotsenburg, about fifty miles north of Manila, but the ships containing their supplies, equipment, and airplanes had not yet arrived. Until the ships arrived, they were going to be billeted at Fort McKinley, an infantry post on the edge of the city.

In the army, there were forts and there were *forts,* and Fort McKinley fell into the latter category. It was like nothing my father had ever seen in the States—lush, green, tropical foliage provided a picturesque backdrop for sparkling white barracks, which were one-story affairs with screened-in porches surrounding them. There was a huge parade ground and a striking golf course. The soldiers all wore white or khaki uniforms. Everything looked clean and felt clean.

Ten men were assigned to each barracks, and my father found himself bunking in the same unit with Conner and Cowert. Along with his two buddies, my father spent the next ten days—the last ten days before the outbreak of war—unloading ships that kept arriving in port; the nights were spent taking in the sights of Manila. My father took rides in *caratellas*, which were rickshawlike vehicles pulled by the tiniest horses he had ever seen; visited the walled city built four centuries earlier by the Spaniards who first arrived in the Philippines; toured the historic rusted hulls of ships that had been sunk in Manila Bay during the Spanish-American War; and went shopping for Christmas presents for my mother—Christmas presents which would never arrive. By the time the fateful weekend of December 7 arrived, the outbreak of war was still the furthest thing from my father's mind.

He went to the Santa Anna dance hall on Saturday night and danced to loud honky-tonk music on a dance floor where nearly a thousand people were able to dance without bumping into one another. On Sunday—the day before the Japanese bombed Pearl Harbor—then-Lieutenant Rocky Gause spent the day unloading ships and spent the night eating, drinking a few beers, and betting on games at the Jai Alai Palace. He returned to the barracks around midnight and went to sleep.

It is important to remember that Pearl Harbor and Manila are on opposite sides of the international date line. Although the Japanese attack on Pearl Harbor took place on Sunday, December 7, the date in Manila was Monday, December 8.

The attack on Pearl Harbor was but one of a series of

nine Japanese attacks planned for the same day, attacks aimed at strategic British and American military installations throughout the Pacific—Guam, Wake Island, Singapore, British Malaya, Burma, Thailand, the Dutch East Indies, and the Philippine Islands. All of the attacks proceeded according to schedule except the one aimed at the Philippines.

General Douglas MacArthur, the commander of the American army and air forces stationed in the Philippine Islands, felt that war was coming and believed he knew *where* it would come and *when* it would come. Theorizing that the ousting of the American forces from the Philippines was the primary goal of the Japanese, he believed the first attack would be an amphibious one aimed at the beaches north of Manila, but thought it was still a good four months off, estimating it would take place in April of 1942. Since MacArthur planned to attack the Japanese troop ships enroute and bomb them out of the water before they reached shore, he never gave the attack any chance of success.

The message arrived in Manila at 3:00 A.M. on December 8, 1941: "Air raid on Pearl Harbor. This is no drill."

The commander of the Pacific Fleet in Pearl Harbor had sent the message to Admiral Thomas Hart, commander of the Far East Fleet in Manila. Admiral Hart passed the message along to the naval officers under his command, but didn't pass the message along to MacArthur, who remained fast asleep in his penthouse apartment in the Manila Hotel.

At 3:35 A.M., the general's phone woke him. It was his chief of staff, General Richard Sutherland, calling. A soldier who had been listening to a California radio station had heard about the attack on Pearl Harbor and relayed the word up the chain of command.

MacArthur reached headquarters at 5:00 A.M. At 5:40, he received an official cablegram from the War Department in Washington advising him that the Japanese had attacked Pearl Harbor—and warning him that the Philippines might be the victim of a similar sneak attack. Actually, the Philippines should have already been the victim of a similar sneak attack. Four hundred Japanese bombers and fighters were sitting on runways on the island of Formosa, three hundred miles north of Manila, waiting for the order to take flight. The only thing delaying them was a heavy fog.

That fog afforded MacArthur time to prepare a defense of the Philippines. Moreover, the fog afforded MacArthur an opportunity to beat the Japanese to the punch by launching a preemptive counterattack of his own.

For unexplained reasons, General MacArthur did neither.

My father woke up a little after 8 A.M. on December 8— Black Monday as it came to be known in the Philippines— planning to do the same things he had done the day before: unload ships and go to jai alai. After showering and dressing, he went to the mess hall for breakfast and ran into Lieutenant Cowert. As they were eating, they heard an emergency broadcast come over the radio: Pearl Harbor had been bombed by the Japanese. The announcer did not know the extent of the damage, nor did he know if the United States had as yet declared war on Japan, but he did instruct all U.S. Army personnel to report to their bases of operations as quickly as possible. For my father and Cowert, this meant the officers' club, where a reconnaissance headquarters had been established.

They ran to the officers' club and were about to enter when they bumped into Lieutenant Conner, who was racing out the door. Conner told them he had been ordered to establish a communications depot and to have it up and running within three hours.

The three of them looked at one another. That was an impossible task. To begin with, where was the radio equipment? As far as they knew, most of it was in the port area, either still inside the hulls of ships or downloaded into the backs of trucks which were parked all over the place. Even if they found the equipment, who was going to operate it? The rest of the men in the unit could be anywhere— sleeping, playing golf, or still in Manila from the night before—many of them unaware of the attack on Pearl Harbor and in no hurry to return to base. And where exactly were they supposed to set up this depot?

They rushed back inside to get additional information.

With more than a hundred officers scurrying about, the main focus was a long table in the center of the room where the top brass were sitting on tall stools, pushing model airplanes around a large map of the Pacific. By then, the fog had lifted over Formosa, and Japanese aircraft were now headed toward the Philippines.

Unable to find the colonel who had given him the order, Lieutenant Conner found a general who confirmed it: Round up all available communications personnel, set up a bivouac at the firing range south of the fort, and get on the air by noon. Their duties specified, Conner, Cowert, and my father formulated a plan: Conner would locate the men, Cowert would locate the supplies, and my father would locate the equipment.

Somehow Conner found all thirty men; Cowert found tents, cots, mosquito netting, food, and two cooks; and my father found two radio transmitters and two receivers. More remarkably, they regrouped on the firing range south of Fort McKinley within the allotted time, and my father established a communication network that stretched from Manila to Hawaii in one direction and from Manila to China in the other.

No sooner had my father completed the task when he looked up into the sky and saw airplanes, so many he decided to count them—seventy-two in all—bright and shiny in the noonday sun. Even though he had seen his superior officers pushing tiny plastic airplanes around the map of the Pacific a short while earlier, it never occurred to him that these airplanes could be Japanese. He thought they belonged to the navy and believed they were being deployed in some sort of defense maneuver. And that's what he kept thinking, right up until the time he saw hundreds of shiny little objects dropping out of their bellies, objects that sparkled like aluminum chewing-gum wrappers as they floated earthward, slowly and silently at first, then faster and whistling as they got closer to the ground, until the whistling grew so loud it filled the air with an ominously shrill sound.

Hitting the dirt just before the first bomb exploded, my father felt the earth shake beneath him and heard the screeching of shrapnel flying through the air above him and the rumble of buildings crumbling in the distance. He hugged the ground until the shelling stopped several minutes later, stood up, looked into the sky, and saw that the enemy aircraft were heading off into the distance. Surveying the damage, he saw destruction everywhere—buildings without walls, without roofs, many of them on fire—so much destruction he knew there had to be a great number of casualties and deaths. Only then did it sink in that he had just been bombed by the Japanese, yet had somehow survived.

The same thought occurred to everyone else at the same time. Smiles formed on their faces and everyone was cheering and jumping, laughing and yelling, shaking hands and slapping one another's backs—that's how glad they were to be alive. After the mini-celebration ended, my father sent a radiogram home to my mother: "Am alive and giving them hell—Rocky."

As soon as the first bombing was over, headquarters called with new orders: Tear everything down, move to the other side of the fort, and resume transmissions as soon as possible. They did all of this, but a problem soon arose. They had started out with five trucks, but only four arrived at the fort's other side. Someone had commandeered the fifth truck, the one containing the kitchen supplies and the food. This would create a severe problem in the days ahead.

Unlike at Pearl Harbor, the Japanese did not stop in the Philippines after one attack. Constant aerial bombardment followed for days, destroying most of the Allied aircraft and damaging or destroying most of the antiaircraft installations. As a result, subsequent air raids proceeded virtually unchallenged, forcing my father's crew to remain on alert around the clock, with little or no sleep, and no food. To alleviate the food problem, Lieutenant Conner made food runs to the mess hall or into Manila, sometimes taking my father with him. During one of those runs into Manila, the Japanese launched an attack. As my father ducked for cover, he came face to face with a young Filipino woman lying in the street, bleeding. With bombs bursting all around them, he picked her up in his arms and carried her to the hospital. He thought nothing of it at the time, but she never forgot. After recovering, she sought him out and thanked him for saving her life. Her name was Rita Garcia and, in a remarkable yet fitting turn of fate, she would reciprocate a few months later by saving his life.

Three days after the initial attack, my father's group received orders to move once again, this time to the control tower in the center of the airstrip, the only building left standing and a prime target that fell under attack night and day.

Every time the Japanese attacked, Lieutenant Buzz Wagner climbed into the cockpit of the lone P-40 left to defend the fort, and my father and the rest of the men in the tower came out and cheered for him. The routine continued for several days, until Wagner engaged in a dogfight and was wounded as a burst of enemy gunfire spattered his windshield and left him with a faceful of broken glass.

Completely defenseless from that point on, my father's crew took cover every time the Japanese planes swooped in to attack, the enemy machine guns blasting and bombs exploding everywhere. For two weeks, my father's crew experienced one close call after another but somehow avoided a direct hit.

While the aerial bombardment continued, eighty Japanese troop ships were steaming toward the Philippines. This was the amphibious force MacArthur had anticipated. But with most of the Allied aircraft destroyed—only three B-17s and a handful of P-40s remained—MacArthur lacked the firepower to thwart the impending attack.

On December 22, the troopships reached the Philippines and disgorged 43,000 Japanese soldiers onto the beaches north of Manila. The enemy's inland advance came so swiftly and so powerfully, there was no time to move the supplies that had been stockpiled near the beaches. Rather than have thousands of tons of precious food, medicine, fuel, and ammunition fall into the hands of the enemy, General MacArthur ordered everything burned.

Once again, my father's crew received new orders: Pack up, report to Pier 7, load everything onto the first available boat, barge, or ferry, and sail north across Manila Bay to a docking area halfway up the Bataan Peninsula. There, they would transport the equipment four miles inland to Little Baguio, a crossroads in the middle of the Bataan Peninsula, and resume transmissions.

It was 2 A.M. by the time they packed their gear and arrived at the port, so they decided to sleep in the trucks. But come first light, they found hundreds of soldiers and vehicles in front of them waiting for the handful of boats that were docked in the port. Making matters worse, daylight also signaled the return of Japanese planes dropping bombs and strafing at will.

Rather than have his men remain sitting ducks, Lieutenant Conner requested and received permission to drive to Little Baguio, a landmark so small it wasn't on the map, even if they had had a map. Bataan itself was a mountainous jungle peninsula, some twenty-five miles long and twenty miles wide, mostly uninhabited, where famous circus performer Frank "Bring 'Em Back Alive" Buck had once captured the largest python in captivity.

Since none of them had ever been to Bataan, let alone Little Baguio, they neither knew where they were going nor how to get there. They did know that they needed to drive to the town of San Fernando, about fifty miles north of Manila, then find the only road leading to Bataan. They also knew that the Japanese army was advancing rapidly and had to pass through San Fernando to reach Manila. If the enemy beat them to San Fernando, the risk of being shot, killed, or captured ran high.

Hoping to expedite matters, Conner decided to trade the trucks in for cars. After ordering half of the men to stay behind to guard the trucks, he took the rest with him to roam the streets in search of abandoned vehicles. He and my father found two 1940 Ford sedans parked in front of the Hotel Manila, and the rest of the men were equally successful, locating another dozen cars. While the equipment was being transferred from the trucks to the cars, my father and Conner went to search for food.

Around noon, fourteen cars rolled out of Manila, with my father and Lieutenant Conner in the lead car, but progress was slow. Cars, trucks, buses, and *caratellas* jammed the road, along with men, women, and children on foot, carrying as many of their worldly possessions as possible.

It took all day to reach the outskirts of San Fernando, where the sounds of the approaching Japanese army were audible in the distance. With no time to waste, they drove through town, found the road to Bataan, and cleared San Fernando before the enemy arrived.

On the other side of town, they outdistanced the pedestrians but still found the road clogged with vehicles. With more stops than starts, top speed never reached fifteen miles per hour, and the ever-present threat of air attack necessitated that traffic proceed under blackout precautions.

A few miles south of San Fernando, traffic came to an abrupt halt and refused to budge for a good half hour. Growing impatient, a driver in one of the vehicles behind them started honking his horn and yelling, then turned on his headlights. Since this put everyone in jeopardy, my father got out of the car and walked back to the vehicle in question, a large yellow bus, and asked the driver to turn off his headlights. After the driver complied, my father returned to his car.

Several more minutes passed without movement, then the honking and yelling started anew, along with the headlights. Once again my father walked back to the bus, this time warning the driver that he was going to shoot the headlights if he didn't turn them off. Again, the driver complied.

But less than two minutes later, it happened a third time.

Taking a rifle with him and without saying another word to the driver, my father aimed at one headlight and fired, and then the other. He accomplished two things in the process. One, he turned off the headlights for good. Two, the shooting started traffic moving.

But progress remained slow, and they drove all night without nearing their destination.

At daybreak, the air raids resumed. Seeking cover, my father's convoy pulled off the road into the jungle and the soldiers spent the day sleeping. After nightfall, they resumed the drive and succeeded in finding Little Baguio, where they pitched camp, set up their equipment, and cooked dinner. By then, it was Christmas Eve.

Christmas Eve was also when General MacArthur evacuated his headquarters in Manila and moved to Corregidor, a rock island fortress guarding the mouth of Manila Bay. Earlier that day, the Japanese had launched a massive amphibious landing south of Manila. Realizing that his army was about to be caught in a gigantic pincer movement, MacArthur ordered a full-scale retreat to Bataan.

The retreat was successful, but there were soon 78,000 troops trapped on Bataan, running low on food and ammunition, along with 26,000 starving civilians. With Japanese soldiers pressing closer and closer, the Americans and Filipinos were doomed to defeat—and more than half of them were doomed to die.

Yet the Allies fought valiantly for nearly thirteen weeks.

On the evening of March 11, 1942, General MacArthur addressed the troops by radio from Corregidor and made his historic "I shall return" speech. That night, by order of President Franklin D. Roosevelt, MacArthur left Corregidor in a PT boat, then boarded an airplane bound for Australia, where the president wanted him to regroup and to prepare a counterattack. Little did anyone know at the time that it would be two years before MacArthur returned to the Philippines.

FOR MY FATHER, the period between Christmas Eve and New Year's Eve had been peaceful. Far removed from the battle being waged for Manila, he felt safe for the first time since the war began. The only problem was the chronic shortage of food. To alleviate the problem, he made several trips to Manila, the last one taking place on the afternoon preceding New Year's Eve. He succeeded in finding enough food to last his unit for several days and was in the process of loading it aboard a truck when Rita Garcia appeared. She thanked him for saving her life and, since it was New Year's Eve, she invited him to join her at a party later that night. After delivering the food to Little Baguio, my father returned to Manila with Lieutenant Conner accompanying him.

This is where my father's journal begins—as he and Lieutenant Clay Conner walk into the Empire Room of the Manila Hotel three hours before midnight on New Year's Eve of 1941. With the exception of minor editing to correct spelling, punctuation, and syntax errors, what appears in this book are the exact words my father wrote more than fifty-five years ago.

—Damon Lance Gause, 1999

THE WAR JOURNAL

OF MAJOR DAMON "ROCKY" GAUSE

CHAPTER 1

IT WAS INDEED A strange sight. I doubt if the Empire Room in the Manila Hotel had ever been host to as varied a conglomeration of people. The Japanese were expected in Manila within a few hours, so the bars were down. And the bars were well patronized. I thought of the boys digging in on Bataan. They would never believe that I celebrated the approach of a New Year—and the Japanese army— from a front-row seat in the doomed city. Everybody danced that night, young and old. Against the distant rumbling of big guns the music was loud and occasionally off-key. People were drinking too much, more than they would have normally. There were little parties in progress around the velvet-walled room and there was much loud talking and raucous laughter as people tried to forget. This was more than an ordinary New Year's party. We were commemorating the passing of an era as well as a year.

Clay Conner and I were definitely out of place. Pistols swung at our hips. Our G.I. brogans hadn't been shined in weeks, and we hadn't shaved since leaving Fort McKinley for Bataan on Christmas Day. Our khaki shirts and trousers were filthy. We were the only American soldiers

1

in the place. In fact, the only men there in uniform, unless perhaps a Japanese reconnaissance patrol was snooping around. We would have been on Bataan with the rest of our forces, if we hadn't been ordered to return to Manila for badly needed radio equipment that had been forgotten in the evacuation rush.

One of the little Filipino waiters was busy changing our plates.

"Will you give the Japanese as good service as you have us?" I asked, half jokingly, half seriously.

"Oh, but I will not be here then," he answered quietly. "I am staying only until there is no further need of me tonight. My gun is ready in my room. By dawn I will be on my way to Bataan."

"You might do better if you stayed here," I told him. "It isn't going to be any picnic on Bataan. And you don't have to fight, you know."

He drew himself up to his full five feet. "Sir, my brother was killed five days ago in northern Luzon. My father is in the hills, fighting with his old outfit. My mother and sister have gone to care for the wounded. We will fight, all of us, to the end."

"But the Japanese say they are bringing you freedom," broke in Conner. "They may treat you well."

"The Americans have promised us freedom. It is their kind we want. We will never forget what they have done for us. And the Japs we will always hate."

His last words were said in a tone that sent a shiver down my spine. He meant every word. I wondered if all his countrymen felt that way. Through the long months ahead I was to learn that they did. I have often wondered what happened to the boy and if he is still fighting "to the end."

Conner and I were at the hotel to join Rita for the last time before we pulled out of the city. We had seen her by chance on Escolta Street early that evening. We had been loafing along, after loading our trucks with the radio equipment and supplies that were hidden in the Santa Anna cabaret. I had told the men where we would meet an hour before dawn to begin the trek back to Bataan. Then Rita had come rushing across the street to thank me again for saving her life. Again I told her that I hadn't saved her life, that anyone finding her wounded would have picked up and carried her to the hospital. But she insisted that I had, and asked us to her home. We had nothing to do and the "last day and inevitable hour for Manila" atmosphere that pervaded the city wasn't exactly cheering, so we accepted.

She had taken us to a rambling Spanish-type hacienda, in a good residential section, where her mother, her younger brother and two sisters were almost overwhelmed at the prospects of the invasion. Her father was with the Filipino army in the heavy fighting in the north, where the Japs had first landed, and nothing had been heard from him. The family feared he was dead. The purpose of the visit was to persuade me to take the mother and young girls to Bataan when I returned. I explained how impossible that was. Then she suggested that Conner and I meet her at the Manila Hotel.

When she came across the room to our table I realized again how charming she was. Her long black hair framed her sparkling eyes and cameo-like Spanish features. Her evening dress was dark red studded with sequins. She looked very different from the first time I had seen her on the roadside, but if anyone had told me that she would be wearing a sarong when we finally said good-bye I would have said he was bomb-happy.

Rita danced with Conner and then I asked her to dance. My muddy shoes sank lusciously into the heavy carpet as we picked our way between the overcrowded tables and milling patrons toward the postage-stamp dance floor. Rita spoke to many people and asked one girl if she wouldn't like to go over and sit with Lieutenant Conner until we returned. Things like that were being done in Manila on December 31, 1941. The orchestra was playing "The Beautiful Blue Danube" as we began jostling our way around the dance floor.

I expected Rita to begin again the plea that we take all her family to Bataan, but she didn't mention the subject. Instead she told me that she had graduated from college only the summer before and that her father, who had a business in Manila, hadn't been home since December 8th.

She asked a few questions. I told her that when the Filipino and American forces pushed across and around Manila Bay to Bataan, I had remained at Fort McKinley to destroy the radio stations, then had led a convoy to the peninsula, and returned for more supplies. She could not understand how I, a pilot, was now working with radios, but I explained as best I could that when we had no more planes to fly, I had been placed in command of the communications section. The music ended then, and we rejoined Conner and his friend.

"Miss Rodriguez, this is Lt. Gause," Rita said simply,

and we all had another drink. Several more people joined us and we had a lively party until about three-thirty, when we called for the check. A silly thing to do I thought, with the Japs only hours away. The management had decreed that the party was "on the house," however, so we thanked the waiter and left the still bustling Empire Room with the strains of the Philippine national anthem ringing in our ears.

The marble pillar lobby of the Hotel Manila, where General MacArthur had made his headquarters, was quiet and deserted and our heels clacked ominously on the shining floor as we walked towards the door. The battered blue Hudson sedan, dirty and dented, that I had picked up in Manila and driven to Bataan on my first trip, was parked majestically at the main entrance. The three of us lit cigarettes and rode in silence through the darkened streets. Rita was sitting between us in the front seat, and I felt her shoulders heave spasmodically a few times. I saw that she was crying. It was the only time I ever saw her cry, although she was to endure many hardships. She still hoped I would save her mother and sisters from the ravages of the victory-maddened Japs, but Clay and I left her forlornly at the door of her home and returned to our rendezvous.

Our small, four-truck convoy was to move out of Manila just before dawn, along the road that skirted Bataan Bay, through the town of San Fernando at the northern tip, and then into Bataan. When we had all assembled, Col. Jack Sewell, commander of our dive-bomber group, rushed up, driving a staff car, and said that he had come into the city to notify me that a ship would be anchored off Bataan in the morning to take a group of pilots to Australia. We had all been hoping for such news and I delightfully prepared to begin the trek to Bataan. Several days later, however, I saw the ship that was to have carried us to Australia with its masts barely sticking above the water in a bay off Bataan. The Japs had scored two direct bomb hits.

The return to Bataan was a nightmare. As long as there was no hum of plane engines, we crawled along about ten miles an hour with blackout lights. It was impossible to see very far ahead and we drove into tree stumps and shell craters, and were on and off the road scores of times. The blue Hudson was followed closely by the loaded army trucks, and when the sun rose our clothes became drenched with perspiration and dust caked our faces and hands. The radio in my car blared though nobody listened. Two soldiers sat on the roofs of the trucks watching for low flying, strafing Jap planes, and whenever they sang out and beat with their fists on the metal roofs, we jarred to a stop and leaped for the cover of nearby jungle undergrowth.

There was little traffic on the road now, although large numbers of Filipinos, sometimes entire families, struggled toward Bataan hoping to obtain protection from the Japs. Trucks and autos that had broken down lined the macadam strip and we had to make frequent detours around stalled vehicles, bomb craters, and bridges that had been blasted out.

We could hear the crackling of Jap rifle fire as we reached the northern end of the bay, and when we passed through the deserted village of San Fernando we heard the shouts of advancing Nip soldiers. I nursed the car along with a prayer and hoped that the trucks would hold out. I expected that when we crossed the San Fernando bridge a

Jap patrol might step out in the road and open fire. From the village on down into the peninsula the road dwindled into a trail recently covered with crushed rock. Dust was so thick along and above the road that at times I was forced to stop to catch a breath of fresh air. The owner of the Hudson, if he were still alive, would have wrung his hands if he could have seen his battered car.

About nightfall we encountered American troops, this time much more coordinated and settled than they had been when I reached Bataan on December 26th. We were ready now for the grim business ahead.

Weeks later on Bataan, I met Captain Pat Burns, who had left Manila that same morning fifteen minutes after our convoy. He said that when his car loaded with officers reached the bridge in San Fernando a small party of Japs opened fire and he was the only one to escape. He returned to Manila ahead of the Japs and a native sailed him across the bay to Bataan.

Our convoy, therefore, was the last to get safely out of Manila.

CHAPTER 2

CONDITIONS ON BATAAN WERE far from desirable, and before the peninsula was surrendered, I wondered many times how it was possible to live in the face of the steady Jap bombing and shelling. A sturdy mountain range jutted out of the center of the peninsula, and our forces established a line designated at the "Abucay Hacienda Line" because it passed from the mountains to the bay through a town by that name.

Due to lack of trained infantrymen in Bataan the Air Corps men and officers were organized into an infantry regiment. We defended the sector between Manila Bay on the right to the foothills of the central mountains on the left, a frontal distance of approximately 30 kilometers. This regiment was made up of the following Air Corp units: 17th Bomb Sqdn, 16th Bomb Sqdn, 91st Bomb Sqdn of the 27th Bomb Group, the 27th Materiel Sqdn, 7th Materiel Sqdn, 2nd Observation Sqdn, 48th Materiel Sqdn, and a Headquarters Sqdn, of which I was a member during the last days of the campaign. Upon returning to Bataan I was given command of a machine-gun company, which was formed out of the 17th Bomb Sqdn. Utilizing the air-cooled machine-guns that we brought from the States to install on our Douglas Dauntless dive-bombers (A-24s), which never arrived, we established ourselves to defend our allotted sector of the line. I would swell with pride as I watched these skilled men lay aside their tools, bombsight, radio, delicate instruments, and pick up a .30 caliber rifle or dig a machine-gun emplacement as if they had been trained in the infantry for years. I never heard a complaint from these men during the bloody days that followed. The first thing we did after setting up our guns was to get in some rifle practice. We accomplished this by picking out a haystack or corn shock and seeing if we could set it afire with tracer bullets. After a few days these men who had never had a rifle or hand grenade in their hands before they came to Bataan were acting like seasoned infantrymen.

In this company I had 20 or 30 expert aerial gunners who formerly had ridden in the cockpit of the dive bombers with us. These men I put on the antiaircraft 50's we had. One of these men, Pvt. James Oestricher, an aircraft sheet metal worker by trade, improvised a pair of .50 caliber guns on a carriage which looked something like a coaster wagon. Oestricher would pull this contraption behind him wherever he went. He built a dummy haystack which he would set over his guns. When the dive-bombers peeled off to dive, Oestricher would scramble for his emplacement, throw off the haystack, and open fire point blank at them. He was accredited with two Jap dive-bombers within a period of three weeks. Oestricher was only 18 years of age. He was from Quitman, Georgia. Yes, he made a wonderful record for himself and the Air Corps. About two days before Bataan fell, Oestricher was killed by a direct bomb hit that was dropped from a plane as he fired point-blank at it.

We were fortunate that for the first two or three weeks the Japs didn't make a strong assault on our sector. The only ground action we had was when a patrol of about 18 Japs tried to penetrate our lines during the early morning. The men got in some much needed rifle practice on them, and after about a thirty-minute skirmish all 18 were riddled. This little instance gave the men confidence in themselves and their new weapons (the rifle). After that it was hard to get them down. They wanted to advance into enemy territory and look for trouble. Thereafter whenever scouting parties were organized to scout the enemy several miles behind the enemy lines, there were always more hands raised than men needed for the job.

Our men were on the alert at all times and that was tiring. Finally by strength of numbers, the Japs broke through along the bay side and the American and Filipino forces fell back to a previously prepared defense sector from Orion, on the bay, to Bagac, on the China Sea. Here we had a continuous line girding the peninsula and made our stand for all but a few days of the campaign.

The first week in January brought the first heavy Jap attack on this front, during which an estimated 15,000 Japs were killed or wounded. I was commanding a machine-gun company boasting twenty of the best aerial machine gunners in the army. They had mounted their air-cooled caliber 50s on makeshift tripods and piled the Japs, one on top of another. After the first big push, which failed, the Japs contented themselves with constant bombardment and occasional skirmishes.

Our Air Corps men soon learned the tricks of the infantry trade and became as much at home in a slit trench or foxhole as a professional infantryman. Morale was good, and whenever communications had to be laid into Jap territory for reconnaissance purposes, there were always a host of volunteers.

Early one night, about fifteen of us were stringing a wire to an outlying sentry post when we saw two Jap scouts sneaking away in the underbrush. We fired a volley and brought both of them down. One was killed instantly, and when we ran up to them the other was dying. He was the first Jap soldier in uniform that I had seen face-to-face, and he was the most pathetic and frightened man I can ever recall.

He expected to be bayoneted on the spot, it seemed, but we offered him a sip of water, and it couldn't have reached his stomach before he slumped over. These two were the first Japs the men in our section of the line had killed and when the scouts flaunted the Jap clothing and knick-knacks on their return, everyone felt better. The boys knew now that Japs weren't so tough after all. They could be killed like anybody else.

The heat never let up at any time. It caused us nearly as much discomfort as the Japs. The mosquitoes were no respecters of rank and annoyed colonels and privates alike. It was impossible to sleep without a netting, but you fell asleep when exhausted.

Some nights the men could entrust their foxholes to a pal and slip through the dusk to the communications tent to listen to the radio for a while. By this time, the Japs had taken over control of the Manila station, and the strains of

11

"My Old Kentucky Home," "Home on the Range," and a host of other tunes were being broadcast in the hope that our boys would get homesick and give up. It only served to increase our hatred for the Japs. One night we picked up "Deep in the Heart of Texas" from the States and discovered that it topped the hit parade. Some of the fellows were interested in the fact.

Particularly irritating was a news commentator from KGEI in San Francisco. We listened to him every night for news of the other war fronts, and he never failed to tell the waiting world how the men on Bataan were holding off the Japs and winning skirmish after skirmish and battle after battle. It always left us with a bad taste in our mouth.

Maybe those radio programs initiated some of the wild rumors that made the rounds and caught everyone. There were always troopships filled with American soldiers waiting over the horizon to land fully equipped troops after dark. And American planes were always coming into the three landing fields the engineer units had hacked out of the Bataan wilds. Neither these nor the anticipated supplies ever arrived.

Whenever we went on a scouting mission, I marveled at the ease with which the Filipinos moved through the jungle. The native troops were holding the China Sea side of the line, but some always accompanied our patrols. Two weeks after we dug in on Bataan, one of the scouts who frequently passed through our front line headquarters approached me and said, "Sir, I have a message for you."

I don't know how he recognized me through the beard,

dirt, and grimy clothes. The envelope, he said, had been handed to him in Manila by a girl, and, of course, it was from Rita. She still hoped that we could bring her family to Bataan as she expected the Japs to ransack her home and ravish her mother and sisters at any moment. There was still no word from her father. I was to answer by the same scout, who had been bringing us military information out of Manila, and he would guide them through the Jap lines. Such an undertaking was simply impossible. Should they be picked up by a Jap scouting party there is no telling what would have happened. I told the scout that there would be no answer, and he melted away into the jungle.

From another Filipino scout we learned that the Japs were storing large supplies of ammunition in the town of Balanga, about twelve miles in front of our lines. My men were to establish a forward communications post that night to keep us acquainted by sentry of Jap advances, so I offered our services to Captain Mark Wohfield, whose mission it was to destroy the dump.

We left about dark, each of the fifteen men carrying as many hand grenades as they could stuff in their clothes, and bottles of gasoline with rags twisted into the necks as wicks. It was dawn by the time we reached the poor native village. The thatched huts were lined in rows, and the only sturdy building was a church. Its spire and cross stretched skyward, ignoring the events that were about to transpire.

We didn't see any Japs as we crept up on the windward side, dodging, ducking, and running from house to house, but it wasn't long before we heard the sound of trucks and shouts and noises as if the Nips were unloading the vehicles. A strong wind was blowing and our party retreated to the edge of the village where we held a conference. Lighting the bottles of gasoline, we each took a street and ran up and down both sides, lighting the thatched walls and remaining to make sure that they would burn. In seconds the village was enveloped in flames fanned by a brisk wind. The smoke was dark near the ground, but swelled up in greyish billows, and the crackle of flames was almost as loud as rifle fire. Burning brands carried by the wind ignited huts on the far side of the town, trapping the Japs working in the village, and their cries were rising above the roar of the fire when the stored ammunition began to explode.

After a few staccato bursts it all went up in a tremendous blast, and we leaped up waving our Garand rifles over our heads and cheered. When the embers cooled a trace of a hut still dotted the village site here and there, but the church was miraculously the only undamaged structure. We walked through the debris-littered streets and examined the charred bodies of the Japs who had been working in the village.

Several days later, one of my best friends, Lt. Reid Amron, was leading a patrol through the town, and he asked his men to stop for a minute. He wanted to go into the church to say a prayer. An enlisted man went with him, and the officer just stepped inside the huge Spanish-type portal when there was a burst of machine-gun fire. The Japs had spotted guns in the belfry, sacristy—everywhere in the church—waiting for anyone who sought its quiet. The other members of the patrol hustled to cover as Lieutenant Amron backed out the door, seriously wounded.

The private who hadn't entered the church took Amron under the arms and, holding him almost erect, was dragging him to safety when a hidden Jap machine-gun outfit across the road opened fire, and the lieutenant died in the enlisted man's arms. His body, acting as a shield, saved the private, who was wounded by the burst but managed to fall into a shell hole. The Japs left the officer sprawled in the road in front of the church as bait, but we knew their trick. We sent for reserves, who came up heavily armed and in force sufficient to surround the church. One man volunteered to move forward and draw Jap fire and when the first Jap trigger was pressed, we raked them. Before the fun was over, there wasn't a Jap who could walk away.

CHAPTER 3

ABOUT 80,000 FILIPINO AND American troops and around four or five thousand civilians and their families were on Bataan at this time and by the end of February the food situation was desperate. The men who had been in good spirits and willing to tackle anything as long as they were able to get enough to eat were sick with beri-beri, dysentery, diarrhea, malaria, dengue fever, and even Colonel Irwin Doane, our commander, was ill and unable to get out of his bunk. Still the Japs kept coming on, and the day and night attacks by air were relentless.

I obtained permission to organize an emergency mess to feed the men and officers of at least the regimental head-quarters. The men of the communications section were willing to go into enemy territory to hunt carabao, corresponding to the cow in this country. To this fare, obtained at great risk, we added rice threshed by civilians under guard of a couple of soldiers in the paddies between the front lines. The soldiers were assigned to make certain that we obtained half the rice, as much as to protect the civilians, but by these means we struggled along, and Colonel Doane recovered sufficiently to get up and around before the fall of Bataan. Many of the men, too, regained some of their former strength.

The Japs had burned rice fields behind our lines with incendiary bombs. Some nights the flames danced wickedly in the air. Other paddies in front of us we purposely covered with water, and now they were a bed of muck,which would slow down anyone with ideas about attacking us.

One day I saw a man cooking something beside his foxhole that he insisted was a pig. I knew it was a dog and was inclined at first to reprimand him, but I saw the hollow cheeks and pallor in his face and walked away, saying: "That's a nice color pork you have there," but I refused his invitation to join in the feast.

Monkeys, too, tasted like roast beef to the hungry men, and I even heard of some who shot a python that stretched out in the trees, and made some kind of snake stew.

Near the end of March we noticed that a heavy dive-bomber and artillery attack was being launched on Corregidor. The island had been bombed off and on since the Bataan campaign began, but for four days the peninsula had some respite and Corregidor bore the brunt of the Jap attack. Then they returned to us, and instead of pounding our entire line as they had been doing, they concentrated on the center at the approaches to the mountains where it was hardest to maintain a continuous front.

During those days we were never without the braaam and crash of bombs and shells in our ears, and what had been verdant jungle when we arrived on Bataan was now shattered trees and stumps and trampled grass and underbrush. Scouts hiding in the mountains but in communication with us by field phone and radio had previously been able to direct our artillery with great success, but now our field pieces were sadly in need of repair and ammunition was low. There were no planes to offer any resistance and, after several days huddled in our foxholes, I realized that the end of Bataan was near.

The Filipino troops were struggling valiantly in the line at our side, next to Manila Bay. It was strange that, with bombs bursting all around us, I should think of these little brown boys, about five feet tall, of the 31st Filipino Infantry. Here they were, fighting side by side with us although even we had given up hope of getting help from home. They had taught us how to thresh rice and look for fruit, berries, and other native food—how to stay alive. The future held little for any of us, but the Filipinos all had families and friends in the mountains to whom they could have deserted easily in civilian clothes and escaped all danger, including the possibility of long imprisonment. Yet they stood, solemn-faced, fighting day after day with us. I guess those were some of the things that made the Americans so hard to rout out of the peninsula. We were simply worn out physically and facing tremendous odds in materials and supplies when the Japs finally broke through.

You can't account for things that run through your mind at times like these. I looked at the men crouching in their foxholes, still peering toward the area in which we knew the Japs were patiently waiting for us to starve, and I wondered if the men in the Alamo felt as we did. Or Custer making his last stand.

When General MacArthur left Bataan near the beginning of March we assumed, but wouldn't admit, that the end was only a matter of waiting. I'll never forget the sound of our great general's voice as it boomed out at us from the radio under cover of the Philippine darkness before he left.

"Men of Bataan and Corregidor," General MacArthur said, as leaves and twigs rustled as the men who were lounging in the background sat up or drew nearer to the radio, "after declining to leave you twice before, I have now received orders from my commander-in-chief to proceed to Australia and take command there. Men, I must leave you now, but you have my solemn oath that if God spares me I will be back to stay. Have faith, men! God bless you!"

After hearing our leader's voice trembling with sadness and sincerity, both Filipinos and Americans took their belts up another notch, grasped their rifles a little more firmly, and determined more than ever to make the Japs pay a dear price of blood and bone for Bataan. That had been more than a month ago.

On the morning of April 8th, rumors straggled along the line that Jap infantrymen were pouring through the middle of our Orion-Bagac line. There had been so many rumors up to that time that we were still stuck steadfastly at our posts, but at noon the order was received to fall back. I wondered how we could do it. So many of the men were weak, ill, or wounded. Even today I marvel that any were able to obey the command.

Most of the boys tried to carry too much with them. If they were strong enough to lug a rifle or help a buddy they were fortunate, and Jap souvenirs lined the one good road that wound around the foothills of the Bataan mountains.

The car I was driving was filled with radio supplies, and about every hundred feet a Jap plane roared low, strafing and bombing the line of plodding men.

The wounded and exhausted dropped out of the ragged columns and flopped in the dust. Bleary-eyed men, at least two with an arm blown off and others with blood dried and caked on their battle-stained and torn clothes, wandered dazedly, oblivious to the activity about them.

Late that afternoon the Japs who had been over us continuously for hours expended their last bit of ammunition in the all-out attacks against the scores of targets our retreat afforded. There was insufficient time before darkness for them to return to their bases and refuel and re-arm, so they stimulated strafing and dive-bombing along our column, scaring the stragglers and causing us to dive for cover. There was always the possibility that they would open up, so we invariably hit the dirt. At one place the road wound along the edge of a precipice where there was absolutely no protection against their air attack. Some of our cars and trucks had disappeared over the edge and dropped several hundred feet to absolute destruction, but luckily when my vehicle pushed along the passage, the Japs were reduced, because of earlier ammunition extravagance, to scare attacks.

There had been no food since the previous morning and only the excitement and sheer nerve kept the men moving. We hoped to make a last-ditch stand further on, but we were being pressed so closely that we were likely to be run into the ocean.

The morning of April 9th, I saw that we had to get food or there wouldn't be even a trigger pulled in the impending battle. I pleaded with Col. Doane, who was so weak he could hardly walk, and he told me to go ahead if I thought I could get something to eat. I motioned to Sgt. Wilmer Baker, and we commandeered a ton-and-a-half truck and started for a quartermaster station near the tip of the peninsula. I selected the sergeant because with him I had been very fortunate in obtaining supplies. A few days before we had killed a horse, quartered it, and convinced the men who ate it that it was beef. One was even heard to remark that it was the best beef he had ever eaten.

By the time we started out for food our ranks had been stripped, with the sick and weak men falling out by the score. If they could get food into their stomachs I was sure there would still be hope for many. The Japs were so close, however, that we could hear their barbaric shouts as they murdered helpless men along the road. Some of our boys were encouraged to keep moving by the thoughts of what would happen if they should fall behind. The screams of dying men ringing in their ears were all too realistic reminders.

When our truck arrived at the QM depot, the officer in charge at first demurred, saying that there were supply dumps nearer the battle lines that we were to draw from. The people at the rear were totally unaware of the situation at the front, and the officer in charge was insulted when I told him bitterly that the enemy would probably be eating in his mess that night. They were, too.

Soon after we reached the depot, a disheveled Filipino infantry officer materialized out of the rush of human activity, and clenching my arm, he said: "You've just come from the front lines. Do you know the whereabouts of

President Quezon? Is he safe?" I told the soldier that the president had remained in Manila till he was literally forced to accompany General MacArthur to Corregidor, and then to Australia where he was carrying on the prosecution of the war.

"Thank God!" the officer said fervently, "because if the Japs ever captured President Quezon, the Philippines would lose forever their greatest patriot and the only one who can return the country to normalcy after they are driven out."

Then he hustled away to his job and I pondered a moment on what he had said. I was to find that feeling for Quezon universal throughout the Philippines. In fact, in one native hut, buried in the jungle south of Manila, pictures of George Washington and Manuel Quezon were pinned side by side to the wall. I remained hidden there during the day and the youngest boy in the family, who had reached perhaps the fifth grade in the Manila schools before the family fled the city, told me quietly and proudly when he saw me looking at the pictures: "President Quezon, you know, is the George Washington of the Philippines." That was the spirit typical in the islands. Quezon, like Washington, was first in war, first in peace, and first in the hearts of his countrymen.

When the food was finally loaded, I nosed the truck, a British-type right-side steering job, back along the torturous jungle road. Streams of natives, military vehicles, tanks, gun carriers, and soldiers were plodding away from the front. They gesticulated wildly at the truck they saw heading into the maelstrom and shouted that the Japs were right behind. As long as we didn't see any of the air corps men retreating, we figured that their thin and always moving line had not been broken and that they were still fighting— and waiting for our supplies. What we did not know was that the Japs had outflanked our men.

The steel bridge across the Lamao River was one of the most important links in the slender American line of communications and supply. I drove our truck onto the span and looked blankly at a Japanese gun carrier blocking the bridge exit, only fifty feet away. The Nips were equally surprised to see us and, for a second, neither party budged. I thought, later, that I might have had time to turn our vehicle around and escape.

At least one of the Japs shouted something that we knew meant "Halt!" or "Surrender!" Baker leaped out the left side of the truck and I was on his heels. The Japs stirred from their lethargy and opened up with their forward machine gun, but it was two steps to the bridge rail and we both went over and into the water—twenty feet below. The river was low at this time of the year and bedded with rocks. I don't remember how I landed, but I didn't feel a bit of pain in spite of the rocks and boulders I must have landed on. The sergeant later told me that he felt no pain from the leap either. Guess we were too scared.

Although low, there was still a swift current in the river, and in a few moments we were carried a hundred feet downstream. The Japs were unable to bring their mounted machine guns into play over the bridge rail and, before they could unlimber their rifles and begin shooting, we were beyond the range at which they could hit anything smaller than a blimp. They did try to shoot us, though, their bullets spattering harmlessly into the water and trees that towered canopy-like above us.

It was late in the afternoon when we did our Steve Brodie act, and I have never longed for darkness as I did during the next half hour. The Japs knew that I was an officer, because of the garrison hat I had been wearing, and were anxious to make me either a captive or mincemeat. I had worn the hat ever since I was awarded my wings at Kelly Field and it was a kind of good luck charm. It had been pierced by bullets and flying shrapnel several times on Bataan, but I lost it forever as soon as my feet left the bridge rail.

The squad from the gun carrier quickly divided, a few taking each side of the stream, and a hurried search was begun before darkness closed in. We were only a couple hundred feet below the bridge, hiding close to the bank beneath the protection of heavy overhanging foliage. Sgt. Baker had lost his revolver in the plunge and mine was wet and useless. "How in hell are we going to defend ourselves?" the sergeant whispered. That was the $64 question for which I had no answer.

As the soldiers came closer, cursing and swearing, and hurrying from one open place to another along the bank looking for our heads in the water, we stretched out and buried ourselves in the mud and water to our necks. My heart was pumping violently and my mouth was dry, although I was immersed in dirty river water. The quick footfalls approached, then stopped a few paces away. I imagined a man peering into the gathering dusk. Was he looking in my direction What if I should have to move?

Then he walked on, and his companions hurried right past and joined him.

Soon after, the heavy jungle night swept across the peninsula, but we still heard distant bodies crashing through the jungle. A patrol was coming back up the river, brandishing torches and lights and talking and shouting across the stream. Sgt. Baker and I were afraid to talk for fear one might be listening close by. We burrowed deeper into the mud and pressed close against the bank. Bushes and tree branches dangled in our faces. From 30 feet away, we could hear the searchers' bayonet blades swishing through the brush and water along the bank. They were giving the river zealous scrutiny.

Spotlights were cast upstream every few seconds, and from their strength I knew that in a minute the Japs would be on us. I planned to make a grab at a rifle barrel, pull the soldier into the water, and strike out downstream, holding him for protection. I hoped Baker would escape detection in the melee that would follow.

The bank above my head quivered from the weight of the approaching soldiers. The bayonet steel slicing the water is the most annoying sound I have ever heard. Then they were over us, talking eagerly in Japanese. A white beam flashed straight out across the creek, and a bayonet and gun muzzle poked down into the water a foot in front of my eyes. I watched it hypnotically and was preparing to dodge its slashes, when it was withdrawn and the searchers moved a few feet farther upstream, and another bayonet cut through the water.

They were near the bridge before I dared turn and look at Sgt. Baker. He puckered his nose as if to sneeze, and I bit my heart, but he ducked his head under the water, stifling the urge. All that night, parties of soldiers moved up and down the stream looking for two nice, but not so fat, Americans.

Two things stuck in my mind as the water began to chill my body. I wondered what old Admiral Dewey would have thought if he could see the fall of Bataan. I was certain that the peninsula was doomed, and I knew that Corregidor could not hold out much longer. I thought, too, of my mother who was along in years and probably praying for me. She would always wonder, I thought, how her son died. So I tried to be brave and await the end. I was so certain that this was "the end" that I could feel the cold steel of a bayonet being pushed through my innards.

About midnight, a large group of Japs forded the river just below our hiding place. They were shouting jubilantly, sensing the complete victory, and once on the other side set up their field pieces and began pouring shells into our rear area at random. We could hear their officers shouting commands. In an hour they moved farther down the peninsula in pursuit of the broken and fleeing Filipino and American soldiers.

About four in the morning, there was little noise except rifle and small arms fire. Crickets still chirped in the midst of the holocaust and the inevitable mosquitoes had feasted on our faces. The sergeant and I removed our shirts, I carefully tucked my silver wings into my trouser pocket, we unlaced our shoes and buried them in the mud; then we proceeded cautiously downstream, keeping in the covering shadows of the bank. We hoped to get back through our own lines.

When we drew near the mouth of the river we smeared mud afresh over our faces and began wiggling across a sandbar that blocked the entrance to the bay. The river, when it was low, flowed beneath the sandbar. As we drew upon the bar I noticed how pleasingly warm the sand was. The water was warm, of course, but after lying in it for so many hours, I was shivering. In fact, the sergeant was shivering so hard, I was sure the Japs would see the ripples on the quiet water near the banks. I was to notice many times again the comforting feeling of warm sand after long stretches in the water.

We had crawled a half a block when we heard footsteps sucking into the sand. The rattling of gear indicated about a dozen men, and I felt sure it was a Jap patrol. I instinctively pressed my arms to my side and prayed that I resembled a log. Sgt. Baker did the same, I later discovered, and the soldiers passed twenty feet away, talking among themselves. I didn't look, but from the boisterous sound of their voices and laughter they were not expecting any live Americans to be within miles.

I had been leading the two-man expedition, and when the Japs passed I inched my way slowly backwards. I drew abreast of the sergeant and we both retraced our path into the water. The sky was beginning to turn pink in the east, so we went a little deeper and buried ourselves once again in the mud.

Neither of us had eaten for a day and a half, although our truck was loaded with food when we abandoned it so unceremoniously. Our primary purpose, unfortunately, had been to get food back to the men and then eat. Baker, however, stuck a can of iron rations in his pocket sometime before we reached the Lamao River, and lying in the brackish creek water, we twisted the can open and devoured the contents. Then the shadows disappeared entirely and we settled deeper in the mud, prepared to spend the day. Time never dragged so slowly. We heard great activity above the bank and at noon saw Japs washing their mess kits on the bank of the river within a few paces of us. We planned to wait for night and make another attempt to escape, but the sun moved ever so slowly across the sky to dip into the China Sea. Water lapping gently against Baker's face was the only indication he was within touching distance when I at last whispered, "Let's go!" but the sergeant and I were so weak from lack of food and sleep and lying in the lukewarm water for twenty-four hours that it was a struggle to crawl once more to the mouth of the creek.

When we huddled in the shallow water on the river side of the sandbar, I saw that getting across and into the ocean was impossible. During the day, the Nips had established a bivouac area at the mouth of the river. Several big bonfires were sending up large clouds of sparks, and by moving back to the protection of the river bank and poking our heads up above the bank at intervals, we saw that the warriors were having a merry time. The camp was enlivened by women and everyone was drinking sake and cavorting about like the victory-crazed devils they were. We didn't realize it at the time but they were celebrating the fall of Bataan.

We crept up the stream against the rippling current, slipping along near the bank, and about ten o'clock the merrymakers quieted down. Our plan was to encircle the camp and get back to the beach and Manila Bay. Baker and I helped each other up on the wooded slope above the river, and he picked up a heavy stick. We rested then, both so dirty from the mud that we looked as vile as the Japs. I finally ventured a few steps and saw that our enemies were covering the entire area. There must have been a regiment encamped.

The soldiers were lying on mats, most of them sleeping, and some were covered with a light tarpaulin. They were exhausted from the hard fight and the celebration. The fires had died down, and the snores from the men closest to us were the only recognizable sounds. We had been without water and food for so long that we both must have been slightly insane because in one motion, Baker who had come up behind, and I darted out, and each of us picked up a canteen and returned to the underbrush to flop down and drink long and deeply.

When empty, we laid the cans down carefully, and I beckoned the sergeant to follow me through the Jap encampment, stepping over prostrate soldiers and dodging others. Some turned and looked at us, but none recognized the two dirty and near-nude figures as Americans. We had traveled perhaps three hundred yards in the general direction of the beach and were nearly out of the camp and breathing almost normally, when a harsh voice broke the night with a gruff and strident command to halt—I think.

In a flash I dropped down on a sleeping mat beside sprawling Jap soldiers, and Baker, without any hesitancy, followed my example. I pulled the tarpaulin slowly off the Jap next to me. He gave a groan and turned over, and I covered my head with the sheet. I lay tense, straining every nerve, but the sentry never even investigated and my bed-fellow snored on blissfully. After perhaps an hour I dared to poke my head out from beneath the cover and glance at the sergeant, who was lying on his stomach, shielding his head with his hands.

He saw me crawl away, wriggling a few feet and lying still as if sleeping, and then sliding another few feet. The camp was in deep darkness by this time, and, after another hour, we reached the beach on Manila Bay and waded into the water up to our necks.

We had heard much about sharks and I couldn't shake off the thought of their rows of sharp, even teeth. The water was warm but I was shivering violently and Sgt. Baker told me he also was unable to control his muscles. We were standing on coral, and as the waves pounded in they would throw us against the rocks and jagged bottom until we were cut in a dozen places. Blood attracted sharks, I recalled uneasily. Moving slowly, hiding whenever we could behind rocks, we waded slowly along the Bataan shore toward the tip of the peninsula.

The moon rose about midnight, and Jap patrols ranged the beach, directing searchlights out into the sea, but we followed the beam with our eyes, and just before it would flash across us, we ducked our heads beneath the water.

An hour before daybreak we were near the village of Cabcaben, near the tip of Bataan, where I thought our lines might have been reformed, so we decided to go ashore. As we came out of the water the waves bashed us down innumerable times and in the struggle to reach the beach Sergeant Baker and I became separated. When I missed the sergeant, I recalled hearing a commotion behind me and paddled around a few minutes searching, but I saw nothing in the black water. I was afraid to call because the area was honeycombed with Japs. The sergeant either died from exhaustion or was attacked by a shark, but he made no outcry, fortunately for me. He has never been heard from since.

There were streaks of gray in the east when at last I dragged myself up on the beach, praying the Americans would be holding a line here. I was without shoes, famished, and tired, and my eyes were almost closed from the saltwater. The water, too, had washed into the gashes from the coral, and every bone and muscle ached. If your hands and fingers have ever become puffed and crinkled from immersion in dishwater, you can imagine how my skin looked.

After resting for perhaps twenty minutes on the sand, I staggered up on the beach through a hundred yards of underbrush to a road that skirted the shore. It was littered with household goods, clothing, military supplies, and every other evidence of flight. I must have been slightly delirious by this time. I was able to think only in streaks, and every few minutes the road, jungle, sky—everything—would merge into a kaleidoscopic mess. I was standing motionless and bewildered in the road, immersed in one of my trances, when a Filipino approached and beckoned to me. I rocked back and forth unsteadily, absolutely unable to function, but he led me off the road perhaps a hundred steps to a thatched shed where his wife and two children were resting. Seeing that I was an American, the bronzed little man blurted out that Bataan had been surrendered and that the Japs were everywhere—"All around!" This latter observation with a wave of his arms and widening of his eyes. Understanding somehow—I was unable to speak coherently—that I must get away, he gave me a shirt and his wife brought me food, native rice, and bread. I rested about an hour with them, and my strength returned miraculously so that I was able to thank them before leaving.

I went back to the beach and the water and tried to work my way farther down the peninsula, but I discovered I wasn't as strong as I thought, and I finally came ashore after perhaps a hundred yards. I located a narrow trail and was stumbling aimlessly along it when two Japs loomed up in front of me. They gibbered at me and laughed in my face. They probably were saying very uncomplimentary things about Americans, but I was helpless. Jap fashion, they took my watch—it was useless to me anyway—snatched my ring off my finger, removed two hundred dollars from my money belt, and administered a kick that sent me sprawling into the grass along the trail. They laughed and left. I was mad as hell.

I had been told that the Japs made a distinction between officers and enlisted men after capture, so I sat up, fished my flyer's wings out of my pocket, and fastened them carefully to my shirt. I hadn't moved ten yards from where I had flattened the grass when a lone Jap carrying a rifle with fixed bayonet stopped me. He ripped the silver wings off my shirt as I told him, with as much dignity as I could muster, that I was an American officer. His answer was a slap in the face and he stepped back with his rifle pointed, daring me to act. I thought he was going to shoot regardless of whether I moved or not. Instead he prodded me in the stomach with the needlelike point and kept alternately shoving me with the butt and sticking me, until we reached a clearing where about 300 American soldiers were huddled together in a prison enclosure.

I was given a final mighty push and landed face-first among a group of men who were too sick, exhausted, and weak to even move out of the way of my falling body. These men, I learned, had been there since April 9th— two days—without food or water. They were bewhiskered, ragged, and thoroughly beaten, and in serious physical condition because of continued exposure to the tropical sun. The Jap guards lorded it over these silent, hopeless creatures like slave masters of old, beating some and bayoneting others on the slightest provocation.

I had been there only a short time when a flight of Jap dive-bombers began circling the prison area and I thought to myself, "These bastards are going to eliminate all of us with a few well-placed bombs!" But the camp was on a narrow runway and the planes were readying to land.

It was a hot, stifling day and the dust, even in early morning, rose in blinding clouds covering everything, grinding between your teeth, clogging motors, getting into your hair. I walked slowly through the prison area so as not to attract attention. Men were lying with flies buzzing around and dipping into wounds. The captured soldiers groaned and begged for water, but the Jap sentries stalked past, spitting at them. Several buzzards floated ominously overhead.

The beach road paralleled the runway and carried a horde of straggling Filipino citizens. When the Japs took control of Bataan, their first act was to force all civilians into the interior. Now the Japs were stopping all of them who passed, taking everything of value. It was a disgusting exhibition by these victory-crazed, sadistic devils.

Children clung pitifully to their mothers' skirts, and lines of fear and fatigue marred the usually bland faces. The Japanese demanded many things, and their cruelty and ruthlessness made me turn away. Any Nip whose bayonet was unbloody soon corrected that oversight. They ripped clothing, ostensibly in their search for valuables, but the poor people who were being accosted possessed nothing of value but their spirit. That the Japs could not break or take. A single word of protest was insurance for a bayonet thrust in the belly. Husbands, wives, and children were separated, with one or more members of the family lying dead or dying beside the road. I decided that a Jap prison pen was no place for me.

On the shore side of the prison enclosure was a two-hundred-yard strip of jungle and then Manila Bay. I decided I'd better make a break before the Japs stopped their looting and became fully organized. I spoke to several of the healthiest appearing Americans, inviting them to accompany me. They shook their heads in refusal and said I'd never get out alive, and if I did I'd have to swim to Corregidor. I couldn't blame them. They had performed their duty valiantly, and were disillusioned and sick of fighting a hopeless, one-sided fight.

It was now about eight in the morning. The sentries were careless, considering us a bunch of helpless creatures, and their primary interest was looting the people shuffling past the camp. I edged over toward the runway. One sentry was sauntering along with his back toward me, a hundred yards away. Another was approaching, holding his gun carelessly on his shoulder. My first thought was to try for the gun, but it might not be loaded. As he drew abreast, I glimpsed a sheathed knife at his side. There was not time to plan further. He passed, and I leaped on his back, pressing my left forearm against his throat with all my strength and grabbing for the knife with my right. He twisted and writhed, screaming. At last the knife came free, and I slid it into his back as far as it would go. I felt his body relax and let him drop.

With the knife in my hand I sprinted into the bush. The captured soldiers had watched my act without a sound, but the Jap's cries had brought other guards. As I ran I heard them shouting and crashing through the underbrush behind me. I suddenly had superhuman strength and leaped over boulders and fallen trees with ease. A few shots fired from the rear encouraged me to increase my lead. Jesse Owens wouldn't have had a showing with me on this dash. When I burst out on the beach I picked up a driftwood plank and kept right on running with bounding leaps into the waves. I was a hundred yards out in the water when my pursuers appeared on the sand, and I was already churning the water in the direction of Corregidor, three miles away. They fired volley after volley in my direction, but they fortunately were no better riflemen than other Japs I encountered.

Swimming rapidly, I saw an inter-island steamer halfway to Corregidor that had somehow escaped sinking. I pushed my plank in its direction, and several hours later pulled myself up on the hot and weather-beaten deck. I didn't even bother to conceal myself, but fell asleep where I first dropped. It was late in the afternoon when I awakened with the skin on my back cracked and blistered. Feeling sure that the Japs had forgotten about me, I cut loose a lifeboat, jumped over the side, and clambered in. Using an oar, I pushed off from the steamer and rowed away from its protection when I heard the rat-a-tat of machine guns. Looking toward shore I saw that my friends of the morning had mounted three machine guns on the beach and were taking pot shots at me. They must have seen me crawl aboard the ship, and the only reason I could imagine why they didn't come out after me was that they had wagered on who would kill me. It was the usual Jap conceit.

After a dozen bursts they found the range and soon had punched a score of holes in the lifeboat. One slug took the right oar out of my hand and I decided I'd better go overboard again. I unfastened the other oar to use as a float, and plunged into the bay water. The Japs continued firing but couldn't get a good shot at my bobbing head and flailing arms, so, about sundown on April 11, I crawled ashore at Corregidor. My eyes were nearly closed, and I was bearded, cut and bruised, literally broiled from the sun and water, and entirely spent.

CHAPTER 4

MY NEXT RECOLLECTION WAS of being gently rocked as if I was still being carried up on the crest of one wave and down suddenly into the trough of another. Then I realized that I was in bed and I peered hard through my swollen and half-closed eyelids. I was in Malinta Tunnel on Corregidor all right and a nurse was shaking my shoulder. I felt my legs, and the cuts and sores had been bandaged. The nurse returned and applied compresses to my eyes, and when I opened them a little later at her counsel, I was sure I was in heaven, and not a Corregidor hospital.

Smiling down at me was Millie Dalton, one of my high-school chums. I blinked my eyes and gasped with surprise. It was difficult to focus my thoughts, and I wondered if I had been having a bad dream and was really back in that sleepy little town in Georgia and my mother was trying to awaken me for breakfast. After I sputtered a dozen unintelligible questions, Millie explained patiently that she left Georgia after we finished school and entered the Army Nurse Corp after completing nurses' training. She had been in the Philippines for a year prior to the war. I also learned that I had been asleep for the past 36 hours, ever since I had been dragged in from the beach.

Millie and I talked about home, our folks, and what we had been doing. She fed me broth, and I worked up to good solid food. I stayed in bed for the rest of the day wondering at times how I had been so fortunate as to reach Corregidor. The next morning I felt completely recovered, and persuaded the doctor to get me some clothes and let me return to duty.

Before the Japs unleashed their fury on Corregidor it was a beautiful, dark green, volcanic isle about one-third the size of Manhattan. It was shaped like a tadpole, being high and wide at the seaward end and tapering off to a low point on the bay side—the side where the Nips eventually landed several thousand veteran troops through the shallow water. To the casual tourist who passed Corregidor on a steamer prior to the war it appeared a typical, peaceful native island with its coconut palm fringed beaches, its little white Spanish chapel poised tranquilly on the hilltop, and the American flag flying comfortingly.

Now the Japs in command of Bataan, only three miles away, moved their artillery into the sector, and fired from the protection of the dense thickets and undergrowth one day and moved their positions the next. All the time they had perfect aerial observation of the island fortress because there were no American aircraft to annoy their observation balloons and planes. They even swung an observation balloon almost over our heads and if a man so much as changed his position it was the signal for a barrage of 105 or 200mm guns. The Japs methodically pulverized everything on the island.

I was immediately assigned to the beach defense of Corregidor on the Bataan side, with the Second Battalion of the U.S. Fourth Marines from China under command of Lt. Col. Herman Anderson. I discovered several pilot buddies had already joined the outfit, including Lt. Dick Donnewald of St. Louis, Missouri, whom I had known since Randolph Field days. Dick and I did a little politicking, so that we were given command of a machine-gun company in James Ravine on the north side of the "Rock" facing Bataan.

From scrap lumber we fashioned a crude hut on the edge of the cliff-bound shore, and here we spent many anxious days under a corrugated iron roof straining our eyes toward Bataan for any sign of Japanese activity. We expected them to attempt a landing at any time. We would sit by an old broken window playing two-handed rummy. At the first crack of the Jap big guns on the other side we would carefully lay down out hands and dive prairie-dog fashion for a dugout a few feet away. We became so inured to this procedure that we estimated the exact time it would take a shell to reach us after we heard the explosion three miles away. We played the edge on this time just to break the monotonous routine. Several times when we crept back to resume our game we discovered that the cards had been blown away by flying shrapnel that daily riddled the shack.

The men had hewn a bigger tunnel out of the dirt and rock 20 feet away from our abode, but Dick and I preferred not to sleep inside since the stagnant air and the ventilation were abominable. There was not much sleeping anywhere because, with the first shell burst in our sector, we were all on our way to the various dugouts and tunnels as fast as we could move in the jet-black darkness. It took 13 steps to cover the distance and we made the run so many times that our feet banged down in the same spots each trip. A week after we moved into the hut a shell screamed over just after midnight, and the two of us started for the dugout like automatons. We just about reached cover when a big shell landed directly on the shack, blowing the building and all our personal belongings to Hades and literally throwing Dick and me headlong into the dugout.

A narrow road ran around Corregidor between the shore cliffs and the mountains, and since it was our only communication line, large quantities of ammunition were stored along the road for use in our few remaining batteries. Frequently, Jap shells would fire our own ammunition dumps and if you had to travel the road, which you avoided as much as possible, it was a matter of running past one blazing dump with your eye on the next to calculate its chances of being hit before you got past. It was a game that improved your speed and agility, but we did lose many men from our own ammunition being set off by the Jap barrage.

Along this road in our sector, when I was first assigned to the north beach, was a large mango tree miraculously unscathed by shells. One afternoon, when there was a lull in the fighting I took the knife which I had kept on me since escaping the Jap prison camp and carved the letters "R" "U" "T" "H" on the trunk of the tree. It was the name of the girl whom I had married in October, only two weeks before I sailed from San Francisco for Plum, which eventually was the Philippines. The next morning when I walked past the same spot, I discovered that a shell had blasted the tree off just above my carving but, as far as I know, the tree stub with Ruth's name was still standing when the Japs took possession.

The constant hammering by air and from artillery, and the knowledge that we could do little besides wait for the Japs to make the next move was discouraging. There was little rest. The food was somewhat better than on Bataan but still meager. Rumors continued about the hundreds of American planes that were coming and the transports crowded with American troops that were waiting just over the horizon for nightfall. One young Marine near us cracked under the strain and refused to leave the tunnel. His buddies tried to shame him into a semblance of his former self, but not even the spark of a man could be resurrected. One afternoon in a dark corner near the back wall of the tunnel, he plunged the muzzle of a rifle in his mouth and pressed the trigger. He left a pitiful note asking us not to tell his mother what he had done. But that can happen to any fighting man, and the Fourth Marines were the best scrappers that ever aimed a gun at anybody. The wonder is that more of our men didn't break mentally during those days on the island.

After two weeks I was given a machine-gun company of my own, made up of Filipino troops. We were still at James Ravine, however, and a few Marines were in the group. One morning I was talking with one of the Marines near the entrance of a culvert under the narrow island-girding road when a shell sailed high overhead. The Japs were feeling out the range again so we prepared to duck inside the culvert, the Marine turning his back toward the beach so that we could keep talking.

The next shell burst right over our heads, and a piece of shrapnel the size of a fist struck the man in the back and came out through his chest, leaving an ugly gaping hole as big as a water glass. He fell toward me, pleading, "For God's sake, sir, pull me in!"

I dragged him into the culvert and tore away his shirt and tried to halt the blood flow, but it did not seem possible that he could live more than a few minutes with a hole that large in his chest. He kept right on talking to me, nevertheless, and after ten minutes it seemed that he might be able to stand the half-hour jouncing trip to the hospital. There were a score of Filipinos in the shaft with us and in spite of one of the most severe shellings of the siege, a dozen volunteered to carry the man. I selected four of the biggest who rigged a crude stretcher, and we set out.

Shells burst first in front, then behind us, sometimes several at the same time; but we kept moving and the Marine continued a constant line of nervous chatter. When the stretcher bearers fell out of step he'd shout, "Dammit, can't you fellows stay in step?" The seesaw motion when the carriers walked out of unison shook him excessively, bringing on agonizing pain that distorted his face. He reached the hospital after what seemed hours but was in reality only thirty minutes. The doctors looked wise and did what little they could for the man. We returned to our post, and at nightfall a messenger brought us a note on which was scrawled, "Thank you fellows."

An accompanying note from the doctor said that the marine had lived until about four o'clock, and that his last act was to scribble the note to the men who brought him to the hospital, with a request that it be delivered to us.

CHAPTER 5

DURING THE LAST TWO weeks of the siege of Corregidor, while I was with the Filipino troops and the handful of Americans, we lost one or two men daily through enemy action. Beginning April 29th, Hirohito's birthday, the Japs opened up with an intensive pounding and most of our time was spent buried in foxholes, guessing where the next shell would burst and trying not to think of home and things comfortable. It doesn't take long to get acquainted with a man in a foxhole. Lt. Alberto Arranzaso, a 23-year-old Filipino pilot, was my second in command, and the desires, hopes, and plans we confided in each other from the bottom of a dusty pit would have been exchanged only between lifelong friends in a peaceful world.

The enemy fire was so heavy and continuous that it became impossible to wash, cook food, or even stand up to stretch your legs. There wasn't much food to cook even if we could have operated a kitchen, but our scant water supply, which dwindled day by day worried us. My Filipino cook-sergeant dug a deep hole directly in front of his stove and laid bamboo poles across it. He'd go scooting around in a crouch preparing rice in a dozen different ways and, when he heard a shell screaming in our direction—which was often—he dropped into his hole. It was a brave scheme, but shrapnel continually riddled the cooking utensils, forcing daily repairs or no food.

With the rainy season coming on, we expected the Japs to try their invasion at any moment. When the foxholes filled with rainwater, we stood in the mud and slime straining our eyes in the darkness for telltale moving shadows or sounds that signified boats and landing barges. During the day the Japs poured shells into every part of the island, but concentrated exceptionally heavy fire for a part of each day on each sector. They were softening us up for the attack we all knew would come.

The rain was warm but every possible cover had long since been blown to bits, and there was no protection from the wet. What food we had was cold and filled with dirt. As fast as our men could fix the water pump system, the Japanese would blast it away again. We found that if you let a puddle of muddy water remain still long enough, a good portion of the mud would sink to the bottom and the clear water on top could be drunk. It wasn't good but it was wet and better than nothing.

April 29th is Hirohito's birthday, and the Japs must have planned a big celebration for that day. We didn't know they could train as many guns on the island as they opened up with beginning at 8 o'clock that morning. They used artillery, machine guns, mortars, horizontal and dive-bombers—the works. They maintained that tempo until the island was surrendered. There wasn't a moment, night or day, that a high explosive didn't dent Corregidor and when the bombardment finally let up the once-beautiful island resembled the pockmarked surface of the moon.

There had been no sleep since the 29th bombardment began, and we felt that the Japs were girding themselves for the inevitable assault. Our defenses were pitiful, but every man had his rifle and machine guns were primed for action. The Japs would know they'd been in a fight.

The night of May 4th was sultry and there was an ominous rumbling of thunder that rivaled the artillery fire. I would have given a month's pay for a Coca-Cola. Red-circled planes hedge-hopped at the island from Bataan and began laying a smoke screen close to Corregidor's shore. They were joined by fast, small boats that circled and laid more clouds of thick grayish smoke. It was maddening to watch this activity and have to admonish a gunner for taking a shot at a plane that swooped too low. The attack was coming in the next few minutes, and we had to save everything we had.

The Nips, however, were waging a war of nerves, because on the morning of the 5th they were still screening with smoke, and we could see none of the frenzied activity and assault preparations we knew must be taking place on the shores of Bataan. But there had been heavy fighting and fierce fighting in the dark at the lower end of the island, where the water was shallow and there were wide and easily accessible beaches. Our sector on the northern edge was never attacked by a landing party, but we learned later in the morning that the Japs had put about 2,000 of their best seasoned troops ashore.

They had crossed the water on flat-bottom boats, small

bancas, bamboo rafts—anything that would float—drifting in out of the smoke and fog in the dark, throwing all their strength against the lower edge. Slipping from rock to rock, American-Indian fashion, they established a few positions. As soon as one threw up his hands with a shriek that cut shrilly above the battle sounds and crumpled to the ground, another took his place. They kept coming out of the water in endless ghostlike waves. Their equipment was far superior, but our ragged, half-starved Filipino and American defenders were not pushed back. When the Japs reached our foxholes and gun positions, our boys went at them with whatever was handy, and when the invaders did press forward it was over the bodies of these gallant Filipinos and Americans.

All morning on the 5th, the sounds of battle grew in intensity. We expected a flanking attack because we knew that the Japs were catching hell although advancing steadily. But at noon General Jonathan "Skinny" Wainwright walked out on the battle line and, with tears in his eyes and voice trembling, he ordered the surrender of the last American stronghold in the Far East. The orders were to destroy all small arms and raise a white flag in our individual sectors. Then we were to march our men, disarmed, to their headquarters to await the arrival of our captors.

After the danger, privations, and hardships the men had undergone during the siege, I expected and would have understood had they cheered and rejoiced at the order to surrender. I looked at Manuel, a 40-year-old Filipino who had left his family on Bataan. He had been manning a machine gun. Then there was young Philipe, who had volunteered for every assignment. My eyes roved up and down the loose ranks of unkempt but courageous men. Not one had even the trace of a smile. Some cursed and swore, and a few cried, as they obeyed my order and broke their rifles on the rocks and threw the bolts into the sea.

Leaving their arms broken and useless I marched my company to headquarters, placed them in charge of the first sergeant and went into the tunnel to report to Lt. Col. Herman Anderson and Capt. Pat McMakin of the Fourth Marines. Even then I had completed plans with Lt. Alberto Arranzaso to escape Corregidor, because I knew what would happen to me if the Japs should catch me again, as they had a good description from several sources. The colonel nodded at me when I approached his desk, and I noticed deep lines at the corners of his eyes. I told him about my men and he stood up and said, "Gause, you've done a good job and I'm not telling you to leave but I understand. Bon voyage!"

I saluted, did an about-face, and rejoined Arranzaso in the tunnel. We hoped to reach the mainland and find shelter with his mother in the hills. We were both absorbed in our plans when someone grasped my arm at the tunnel exit. It was Millie Dalton, a frightened Millie Dalton and not nearly as crisp-looking as the girl who nursed me when I reached Corregidor. Another girl, a Miss Kennedy of Philadelphia, Mississippi, was with her. "I'm horribly afraid of what will happen to us when the Japs arrive," Millie said in a rush and her friend nodded emphatically. She wanted me to take them to the mainland, but neither Lt. Arranzaso, who stood quietly by, nor I was sure that we'd finish the journey alive, so I reluctantly refused. When I last saw Millie at the tunnel entrance she waved and bravely wished me good luck. I had never felt so low, but I turned and ran with the Filipino for whatever cover the northern edge of the island might afford until nightfall when we could start for the mainland, six miles across the bay. We hadn't covered a quarter of a mile when we heard motorized equipment, Jap, of course, thunder up to the main tunnel, and then there was loud talking and shouts and screams. We got away fast.

Arranzaso and I at last flopped breathless under the protective shadows of a beach cliff on the northern edge of Corregidor and damned the Japs. They had resumed their bombardment of Corregidor, undoubtedly out of anger because General Wainwright refused to order men on other islands in the Philippines to surrender also. American and Filipino soldiers were standing around unarmed and helpless in the barrage.

About seven o'clock, we ventured out of our hiding place to scout around in the gathering dusk for some means of getting across the bay to the mainland. A short walk up the beach revealed a sluggish-looking native outrigger that had washed up on the sands. It was duly launched, and the Filipino flyer and I were heading into the waves about 200 feet offshore when Japs on the cliff several hundred feet above caught us in the beam of searchlight that combed the water searching for anyone foolhardy enough to try and leave Corregidor. They fired at us, of course, but we were too far out in the sea for their shots to be effective.

When it was quiet again we heard someone calling to us in English from a rock on the shore. I cautioned Arranzaso that it might be a ruse to draw us back, but we paddled parallel with the island and after close scrutiny called to the figure that we would come in for him. The loggy craft hadn't been turned, however, when the man who hollered that he was a Filipino scout was in the water and swimming out to us. We helped him over the side, handed him a piece of plank without asking any questions, then the three of us began making energetic whirlpools in the water, and the outrigger moved faster than it had moved in its lifetime.

I was beginning to think that getting to the mainland would be a cinch when, once again, we were framed in a searchlight from one of the Jap cruisers that continually circled the island to discourage and pick up fleeing soldiers. The cruiser's gun crews must have been at their stations because a shell went sighing over our heads a few seconds after we were sighted, and several more followed, none very close. In the excitement, however, the boat was overturned, and we were unceremoniously dumped into the water. The sailors, probably slapping each other on their backs and telling each other what marksmen they were, promptly forgot us. Arranzaso couldn't swim, I was dismayed to learn, so we righted the outrigger and swung our dripping bodies aboard. We paddled along with the gunwales submerged, but it was a bit comforting to have something beneath my feet after so many hours in the water previously.

The night was dark and the sea was choppy. We headed into the wind and our paddles lifted and dipped, lifted and dipped. Shells and bombs were still bursting on Corregidor and every once in a while one would come sailing over the island—the Japs couldn't always hit the island—and burst near us. Whenever I heard one whistling in our direction I instinctively drew in my neck and hoped that it would keep on going. When dawn broke, we weren't a third of the way from Corregidor to the mainland. Treacherous crosscurrents carried us sideways during the night, and we made little headway in the water-filled boat.

We were debating what to do next when a Jap fighter plane peeled off from a formation and fired a few bursts at us. The bullets spat into the water alongside the boat as the three of us went over the side, and when I came up Lt. Arranzaso's voice rang in my ears.

"I've been hit!"

I swam to him through the heavy swells and grasped his shoulder, while the Filipino scout swam to the boat and obtained two bamboo poles and an oar. The officer had been wounded in the back by a slug, and although it wasn't serious he was bleeding profusely. I kicked off my shoes and stuck a sock underneath his shirt and against the wound to coagulate the blood. I worried again about the blood attracting sharks. We had heard so much about the danger from sharks that the subject was on my mind constantly.

All day the scout and I swam against the wind and choppy seas, pushing the wounded officer whose arms were draped over the bamboo poles. Late in the afternoon, we were several hundred yards from shore, but there was such a strong offshore current and we were so weak that every movement of our arms was a struggle, and we could not pierce the swirling belt of water between us and safety.

It had been more than two days since any of us had eaten and there had been no water for almost 24 hours. The saltwater licked at Arranzaso's wound, but he clenched his teeth and said little. It was becoming more difficult to stay afloat and all of us swallowed large quantities of saltwater. A combination of hunger, thirst, exhaustion, and exposure made me a little delirious, and for the first time I lost hope.

Jap boats passed us, sometimes very close, and we who had so bravely set out to escape the Japs called to them to pick us up. Our cries were ineffectual and nobody saw us. I later thanked God for that. Soon we were just floating, carried by the current, and we began to see figures on the beach, hiding behind rocks and trees. They might be Filipinos, we thought, but then decided that they were Japs waiting for us. We were in such poor condition that we cried out, and at the peak of each swell we lifted our arms to attract their attention so they'd come out and get us. We were having hallucinations, of course, but at the time I was certain that my eyes weren't deceiving me.

About six o'clock, I told the scout to take our makeshift oar and swim to shore and see if he could find a boat and come back for Arranzaso and me. We hadn't the strength to push the wounded man further in the current, but if we could get a boat I was sure we would all reach land. The scout swam away, and I saw him making good progress through the waves.

A short time later Arranzaso gave me his money belt, saying that it hurt him and that if anything happened he wanted me to give the money to his mother. He gave detailed instructions for reaching his home, interspersed with choking and coughing from the water he swallowed. "I'm certain my mother is alive and can help you," he repeated time and again.

I was pushing the crude raft feebly from behind when the Filipino turned to me and blessed himself. He was about four feet away, hanging on the poles when he spoke. I'll never forget the tone of his voice or the words: "Sir, my game is up!"

He hung his head for an instant, then lifted his arms. His wrists hung limp, and his head slipped below the dark water. I shouted his name and made a violent lunge toward the place where he had been. I dove several times searching, but I felt the swirl of the current as soon as I had gone down a few feet, and I knew that Arranzaso had sacrificed his life to save mine.

The shock of the Filipino pilot's heroic act brought me almost back to normal. I swam with vigor for a short ways, and then looked back to see if by chance Arranzaso's head had bobbed to the surface. I saw no sign of the pilot, but a blazing sun was sinking into the China Sea behind Corregidor. Flames leaped high on the fallen fortress, and the fiery streamers given off by the sun were reflected in the water. The sun was unmercifully dramatizing Corregidor's ignominious plight.

I prepared to endure a second night in the water. The shore was only a few hundred yards distant, but to a man in my condition it might have been miles. I dared not look up for fear I was being carried farther away. My arms were thrashing the water aimlessly, and I was about to give up when a knee dug into the sand. My senses and strength perked up ten-fold but I thought my mind had been playing tricks again, so I took a few more strokes with my head down. Then I carefully let my legs drop and stretched my arms downward, and I felt land. I stood up but was knocked down by the next wave, and alternately crawling and walking I plodded twenty feet up the beach and crumpled to the comfortable sand. I remember that it was heavy dusk and that I fell into an exhausted sleep.

CHAPTER 6

A JARRING KICK IN the side awakened me, and there were more sharp blows along the legs and back. I had been lying on my side. Although I opened my eyes, I was still so drugged from sleep that my reflexes were slow in responding, and I fortunately made no movement. I snapped out of my lethargy when I heard Jap voices and men laughing. I had been mistaken for a dead American, I was sure, and in the darkness the Japs were enjoying the sight of another limp white body washed up on the beach. The minute they were standing around me dragged like years and I expected at any moment for one to plunge a bayonet into my "carcass" just to make sure it was dead. But they straggled off toward the north, one stepping across me, his rifle butt slapping me on the back and dragging over my side. Gradually their voices died away on the otherwise deserted beach. This Jap patrol of perhaps twenty men had no semblance of military order.

Every trace of fatigue had vanished by this time, and as soon as I thought it safe, I arose. Each movement brought an ache, and mosquitoes had covered my body and face with livid burning welts. My eyes were puffed and I could barely pry them open, but it was imperative that I get away before dawn, which I knew was not far off, so I moved south on the beach, looking for a pass through the towering and shadowy cliffs that protected the shore.

My intention was to find Arranzaso's mother and give her the money her son had handed me in his last minutes, and I knew that she could help me. I needed clothes, food, and medical attention. I was wearing only my blue denim shorts, and I was so famished that I knew I would soon do something desperate. The first break I discovered in the rocks opened directly into a Jap camping area but there was no enemy activity, and I hastily retreated to search farther south. The murky light of dawn was making everything indistinct along the path I was traversing when I negotiated a sharp turn and saw a little native village with a score or more of thatched houses. On a second look I noticed Jap rifles stacked in the street and a Jap flag hanging limply in the early morning stillness from a pole on the porch of one of the houses.

Then from the shadowy protection of the path my eyes fell on two green bottles and a melon resting on a table beneath a mango tree, four houses down the well-trodden main road of the village. I was beside the table before I could remember the danger, and smashed the melon with a thudding blow against a corner of the table. I scraped out chunks of the melon meat and stuffed it into my mouth with my fingers. I washed it down with swallows of acid-like Jap beer in the bottles, remnants, no doubt, from the celebration of the night before. I ate frenziedly, keeping my eyes on two dogs that were sniffing around me. I was afraid they'd bark and arouse the camp, but they were the least of my worries. Between the huts on either side of me I glimpsed several Nips peering through windows. It was quite light by this time and, thoroughly frightened, I took a long last swallow and walked away, so that another crude building was between me and the Japs. A khaki uniform shirt had been thrown over a nearby porch rail, apparently to dry, so I picked that up and stuck my arms into it, all the while moving out of the camp as fast as I could without breaking into a run.

I'm certain that the Japs in the house saw me, but they seemed to be dull-witted then and on several other occasions, I am happy to report. They didn't even raise an alarm and I could have kicked myself for not finishing the melon.

There were mountains to the south so I took off in that direction. When I got away from the bivouac area and after an hour's walking, I ripped the sleeves out of the Jap shirt and wrapped them around my feet. The soles were cut and bleeding from the sharp stones and thorns, so the cloth covering felt like a pair of fifteen-dollar oxfords. The few mouthfuls I had been able to eat and the beer only whetted my appetite and desire for water. Late in the morning I stumbled on a brook. I was so relieved I fell headlong into the water, and drank and bathed my swollen face and eyes for at least a half hour. I was afraid then that I'd lose the stream, so I walked up the mountain alongside the sparkling water, discovered a few bird's nests, and stole the eggs, and gobbled them, shell and all. They were damn good. Anything tastes good when you're as hungry as I was.

The countryside was teeming with Japs, but they never expected a lone survivor of Corregidor to be wandering around, so they were careless. Whenever a patrol happened along I could hear them crashing through the undergrowth and talking long before they came in sight, and I would hide until they passed. Several small parties of Japs were camped beside the stream and I skirted those areas. The sleeveless khaki shirt and my thin shorts were in shreds, I was scratched innumerable times before noon, but by nightfall I had climbed to the ridge of the mountain and encountered a stream flowing down the other side.

I found a soft spot in a patch of grass near the water and was asleep almost instantly. The mosquitoes must have invited all their relatives to a picnic. When I awoke with the sun in my eyes I was a mass of red blotches, and I had to press my eyelids apart with my fingers to really take a good look at the surroundings. The stillness made me think of boyhood Saturday mornings in the Georgia woods. I drank long and slowly from the stream and bathed my eyes again, tied the worn strips of sleeve around my feet, and began picking my way down the mountain, following the course of the stream.

The day was sunny and lovely and the jungle was thick and green and teeming with wild life and multicolored birds. But I was famished and considered the birds in light of how much food they'd make and not from an aesthetic point of view. Although I thought a lot about how I might obtain food, I was able to find only a few more eggs, which were promptly chewed and swallowed. I became more hungry and wild for food all the time but the Jap knife was my only weapon.

As on the previous day, I dodged Jap patrols continuously. Late in the afternoon the stream crossed a well-traveled road, for the Philippines, but corresponding to a logging road in the United States. I decided that there should be some habitation along such a path, so I left the stream and walked east. This was the worst part of the day for me. The Japs must have been using the road as a supply line because I had to dive for the covering undergrowth every few hundred feet and wait until groups of soldiers ranging from a dozen to several hundred passed.

Sometimes while straining to make no sound I wondered if it was worth it. I struggled with the thought of stepping out into the trail and giving myself up. The odds against my getting out alive seemed so slim that I convinced myself that I was only prolonging my suffering by trying to escape. I even contemplated suicide several times, but I was afraid that if I used the knife I might not do a good job and I'd be lying helpless for hours before I died. I'm glad I didn't have a gun.

Toward nightfall I was staggering half blind, falling now and then, and praying for something to happen. I saw a figure moving down the path, and I crashed into the nearby brush with little of the finesse I had been displaying. The person who was alone approached and stood right in front of my hiding place. I had been seen at least, I knew, and like a cow I stumbled out of the undergrowth and fell on my tormentor. My arms fell across his shoulders and I pushed him back a few feet, but I was so weak I couldn't have damaged a pygmy.

I was like a drunken man; then I discovered that I was being supported. I stepped back, swayed a little, and looked at him. He was a little Filipino boy about 11 years old. He held me by the arms and whispered in perfect English:

"You are an American. Come with me, sir, and I'll hide and help you. There are many Japanese down there just a little ways," and he nodded down the road in the direction I had been stumbling.

I don't recall that I answered him, but I was so happy to have somebody to look after me that I would have followed him to hell. He led me quickly and silently off the main road into a little used cross-path, holding my hand just as if I were a little boy. I don't know how long we had been walking when we entered a ravine, and there was a newly thatched native house.

He took me to a mat and I slumped down. A woman, his mother I later discovered, brought me broth and food and then the little boy helped me into a back room where I flopped on a banig, a Filipino sleeping mat, and went right asleep. I don't know how many days I slept, but at what must have been regular intervals the boy shook me and gave me food. At last I awakened when I was alone, and I took a mental inventory.

Someone had cleaned my wounds while I slept, but I hadn't shaved for at least two weeks, and my beard would have shamed the original Crusoe. I had no clothes to speak of, but I was relieved to find that the swelling in my face and around my eyes had diminished. I lay there for an hour or more trying to recall all that had happened when the little boy lifted the heavy robe that served as a door, and approached me across the mat-covered floor.

I told him that he was a brave boy and thanked him for saving my life. He replied that he was glad to be in a position to help and inquired if I wanted him to shave me. I was tickled with that suggestion, and he soon returned with a straight razor and hacked away until I was as clean-shaven as the day I was born. I was sitting up by this time but still feeling a bit rocky, and the boy, who said his name was Pedro, told me they were just about to have dinner.

Once again there was a commotion at the door and I saw a tray held by someone backing through the door. A girl materialized out of the dusky corner and was standing before me, her eyes intent on the food to keep it from spilling. I straightened up with a jerk and almost shouted, "Rita!"

The girl, startled almost to the point of fright, looked at me, and I thought she was going to drop the tray.

"Lieutenant Gause," she answered quietly as if she didn't want anyone to hear, "I was in to see you a number of times while you were sleeping, but I didn't know you with your beard." Tears of pity came into her dark eyes.

Then she summoned her mother and sister and we chatted. I had met Mrs. Garcia and her family in Manila, but hadn't paid close enough attention to recognize them when I was brought into the new house. Rita had been away at the time. She told me that after Manila fell they had packed up whatever they needed, hired the necessary conveyances, and moved into their mountain retreat, about 50 miles from Manila. Rita also said with a thrust of her chin that her father had been killed while leading a patrol into Jap lines. He had been dead the night we were dancing in the Manila Hotel.

The Garcia hut was a thatched affair with three rooms but it was very well furnished, and the family still wore their city clothes. Rita insisted that I remain in bed until I had fully regained my strength. She said there was a big

Jap encampment less than a mile away from their home, but that their home was out of the way and would probably escape search. She nursed me faithfully and there was nothing I wanted or needed that she didn't give me or at least try to get.

I marveled at the complete transition of the family from urban to primitive life. Mrs. Garcia, who was used to cooking on an electric stove, now bent over a hearth. Water was carried from a stream and in many other ways they had gone back a hundred years, yet I never once heard a complaint. Their deep hatred for the Japs and their treatment of the Filipinos in general superseded any personal discomfort.

As soon as I recovered sufficiently to walk, Rita sent her brother down to the Jap camp with a few chickens to trade for some clothing. He returned with a pair of rubber-soled shoes, pants and shirt, all Jap military equipment, and Rita found a straw hat of Filipino make. Her idea was to make me look as much like a Filipino as possible. The family had enough money to purchase the clothing but they were afraid that if the Nips even suspected that they had anything worth looting, especially money, they would ransack the house.

Rita also thought that some of the other Filipino families, especially the children who were regular visitors, might see me and let drop a careless word that would bring the Japs on the run. So, she decided that I was to spend my days buried to my neck in rice in a shed hidden in a thick glade behind the house. It wasn't too bad although I became cramped. I knew that it was the safest thing to do, and that made my stay in the bin much easier. Either Rita or her brother would bring me food, and one afternoon Rita even sent Pedro to Nasugbu, a few miles away, to buy me some beer and cigarettes. I had a nice little party in my slatted shed where the sun laid down parallel lines, drinking the warm beer and inhaling deeply on the first cigarettes I'd had since leaving Corregidor.

At night I would leave the rice bin, and with Rita usually leading the way we would walk along the jungle paths she seemed to know instinctively. I could feel strength flowing back into my limbs from the good nourishing food and the rest I was getting.

She startled me one night when she turned, suddenly saying, "Oh my Lord!"

I expected to see a Jap or two loom up on front of us but she spoke on in low tones.

"I forgot to tell you that I didn't send the cablegram you gave me for your wife. I put the note in my purse at the table in the hotel after you scribbled it, but the next day the Japs arrived, and when we fled the city I left the purse in my room."

I assured her that she had done the best she could and that I hadn't really expected to get the message through anyway. But for the rest of our walk I wondered what Ruth back in Georgia was doing and if the Christmas presents I purchased in Manila had arrived. She probably believed herself a widow, since I hadn't been able to contact her since the evacuation of Manila.

CHAPTER 7

A FEW DAYS AFTER Pedro visited Nasugbu he sneaked out to my hiding place and said he thought he ought to tell me something he saw in the village. He appeared a trifle timid about starting the story.

There were approximately 300 American prisoners from Bataan laboring under Jap surveillance, rebuilding docks and bridges in the village, according to Pedro. The Japs had been pushing them from dawn till dusk with never a rest and little food and water, and the prisoners were without hats or shirts and were being burned to a crisp by the tropical sun. Those who wilted were either forced back to work or were liquidated; finally a unanimous mutiny blossomed, and as you might imagine, was quickly and bloodily squelched.

The Japs were unable to put their fingers on the leaders of the revolt, but the next morning as the men were filing to the docks to begin work, the Nips selected two second lieutenants and tied their hands behind them at the wrists. While all the men watched the Japs forced the Americans up on a high box, and attached a rope from their bound wrists to a tree limb. Then they pulled the boxes out of the way, and the officers plummeted downward, twisting their arms backwards and breaking them at the shoulders. The captors left the two officers swaying from the tree, within sight of the laboring prisoners through the morning—until the men became unconscious—and then they were stripped, and laid on the ground to be chewed and eaten by ants and other crawling insects.

Pedro said that he had seen the two men staked out side by side, and that several Filipinos who had tried to give them water had been beaten by the Japs. I thanked the boy for giving me the information and then began some heavy thinking. Every moment I was with Rita's family I was endangering their lives and I was not getting any closer to Australia. I had found a glade where I could lie in the sun during the day and the sores on my legs were healing. I was comparatively strong again and resolved to leave the next night.

Rita and her mother begged me to remain with them at least another ten days, but they soon realized I was anxious to push on. I had told them that I planned to sail to Australia and Rita believed I could make it, but Mrs. Garcia shook her head. It was plain that she considered my chances of completing the trip very slim. Saying "Thanks" to these people who had sheltered and nursed and protected me was grossly insufficient, but try as I would the night I was leaving, I could find no more words. They knew how I felt, though, and there was a glistening in all of our eyes. A big lump rose in my throat when Mrs. Garcia put her hand on my shoulder and said, "God bless you, my boy," in Spanish, just as if I had been one of the family.

They had arranged that Pedro would accompany me as

far as the next town, and then he would find someone to direct me along the route to Mrs. Arranzaso's home in the mountains and then to the ocean again. The family had friends inland, and their relatives were many and loyal throughout the islands. The moon was poised above the horizon when Pedro and I left the hut and moved southward along an indistinct path. We had progressed perhaps a half mile when I heard footsteps padding swiftly along behind us, and someone called softly, "Pedro! Pedro!"

Rita appeared on the trail, and the moonlight slanting through the jungle growth, making patches of light and shadow, framed her dark features and long hair. She told Pedro that he was to return to the house and take care of his mother—that she was to guide me. I saw at once that the girl was planning to try for Australia, too, and I protested, pointing out that it wouldn't be a pleasant experience for her, should we fall into the hands of the Japs. She replied that the Japs would find her if she stayed at home, and she deftly changed the subject by telling Pedro once more to leave. The boy obediently started back up the trail and then he turned to me and murmured, "Good-bye." . . . It was a sad parting. I owed my life to Pedro. Young as he was, he was already doing a man's job and assuming a man's responsibilities. When his little shoulders bobbed out of sight around a bend, I said a little exasperatedly to Rita, "Let's get moving."

The girl took off at a pace that was worthy of a seasoned soldier. She was athletic and lithe and moved swiftly, perfectly at home in the jungle or in a luxurious ballroom. She was out to prove that she would not be a burden on the trip. My new guide was wearing low-heeled shoes and a flowered silk dress that was soon to be torn to shreds. A thin suede jacket that had been popular among the younger set in Manila covered her shoulders. Her clothes contrasted sharply with my poor native getup that was intended to disguise me as a Filipino farmer.

We stopped twice that night to let patrols of Japs pass, and just before dawn we reached a clearing where there were a few native houses. Rita went up to one to see if it was occupied by Filipinos, and then she called me. These poor people had recently been subjected to a looting splurge by a nearby Jap garrison and were reduced to literal poverty. Yet they brought out what little food they possessed and shared it with us. Then they hid us so we might sleep during the day, saying that the Japs wouldn't come near the place since they'd already taken everything of value.

All during our wandering on the mainland we heard the same story from the Filipinos. They all gladly shared their meager rations with us, but all had been dealt with harshly by the Japs and had reverted to a life their immediate ancestors would have shunned. The city dwellers who had wealth of any kind had moved to huts in the jungle they called "evacuations," and we were never refused shelter and food by any of them.

If anyone approached while Rita and I were walking, whether it was night or day, we ducked into the brush adjoining the trail. If the person or persons were Filipinos, Rita would talk with them, and they always gave her complete information about the movement of troops, Jap camps, and sentries in the neighborhood. This information was always accurate and detailed, so we were able to avoid stumbling into the Japs, although several times we came in sight of their camps.

Some of the families we stayed with had husbands and sons who were forced to work at nearby camps or on repair jobs during the day, and at night they'd return and tell us all that the Japs had been doing and saying during the day. It would have been a simple matter—and a profitable one—for them to have turned us over to the invaders, but I know that such a thing never entered these people's minds, and I'm certain that our confidence was never broken.

Although the Filipinos are intuitively curious, they never inquired how I, an American Army officer, happened to be traveling alone with a beautiful and highly educated native girl. They knew we weren't married and probably assumed a lot, but I never enlightened them. My prime objective was to return to my outfit and loved ones, particularly my wife, and Rita was willing to make any sacrifice that these ends might be accomplished.

At our first stopping place, Rita obtained additional instructions for finding the Arranzaso home which she combined with the directions the Filipino pilot had given me, and we left at dusk for the mountains. It seemed as though we were walking in circles. A number of times native families would send a young son to guide us to the next logical stopping place, and once in a while, I became worried for fear the boy was going astray, but invariably we were delivered to our next destination. We dodged Japs all the time, and when resting or waiting in a native home for darkness before resuming our journey, Rita would teach me Tagalog, her native tongue. She spoke English and

Spanish fluently, but wisely added that, if anything happened to her, it would be a help if I could converse with the Filipinos.

It was near the end of May when we came in sight of Mrs. Arranzaso's home. She was a feeble old lady who had been living in a comfortable home in the inland village of Naic but had evacuated with friends when the Japs moved in. She was living in a crude hut practically within sight of her old home—and its new occupants.

When I told her that I had known Alberto on Corregidor she immediately sensed her son's fate, and her little frame shook with emotion. Rita tried to comfort her, and when she recovered her composure somewhat, I told her about the lieutenant's weeks with me, dwelling at length on the pleasant events and skipping hastily over the last few hours. She asked no questions but I felt that she was grateful for the information. I related how Alberto, seriously wounded, had sacrificed his life that I might live, and her sobs broke out afresh when I added that he died "while trying to reach you."

I gave Mrs. Arranzaso the money her son entrusted to me. Even though the poor woman needed every cent, she begged me to take half, saying that I'd need it. She was so humble and beseeching that I accepted a few pesos, which pleased her. She told me I was welcome to remain with her until the end of the war, but that would have been a questionable matter with a Jap garrison so close by in the town. She made us a lunch—stripping her cupboard of the remaining food—and that night Rita and I slipped away down the trail we had climbed so laboriously. We moved southward into more wild and desolate country, traveling by night and even during the day. When we could, we rode carabao, and sometimes we went for days without seeing a human being.

We had been carrying drinking water from a beer bottle, and after becoming lost one night in the blackness of the jungle and unable to get our bearings, we decided to ration the precious liquid, agreeing to take single sips at as long intervals as we could endure the thirst. First, Rita would take the bottle and raise it to her lips and then it would be my turn. There was a label on the bottle, and finally I noticed that when Rita finished her turn and handed me the bottle, the water would be at exactly the same level as before she drank. It was then I learned that through the whole night, knowing that I couldn't see clearly in the darkness, she only pretended to drink her share of the water.

At last we stumbled upon a mountain stream, and both of us dropped into the water, face first, and drank and drank. By this time Rita's silk dress was in rags and my clothes were in practically the same condition. We were covered with mosquito bites, and Rita's legs and arms—which had attracted more than one approving male glance at the Manila Polo Club swimming pool—were now slashed and cut. Purplish blotches showed where she had stumbled against rocks and tree stumps. Still, she never uttered a whimper. She was a stirring example of Filipino courage and loyalty.

After seemingly endless days and nights of wandering, during which I once more entertained doubts about my chances of reaching Australia, we finally reached a small native village on the Balayan Bay. We were welcomed by relations of Rita, who hid us in a small hut on the beach while they found and outfitted a small outrigger with the necessary gear and a few cans of salmon and sardines, rice, a little sugar, and several cans of fresh water. I fully believed that I could sail to Australia in the tiny boat, but I was in for a rude shock.

The night before we were to shove off, 300 Jap troops entered the village and stormed about looking for American soldiers they had heard were hiding. We set sail immediately for the island of Mindoro, and it was a sad experience. Rita handled the tiller, and I, who had been reared in the hills of Georgia, tried to operate the sails. I was a pathetic sailor. Only after being knocked overboard several times did I figure out why the sail boom should suddenly sweep across the boat.

When morning came, Mindoro wasn't in sight but we were close to Lubang, which was only about 25 miles from Corregidor. The island was a discouraging sight, but we had to land and I have never regretted it. The next month was the most pleasant of my entire trip, although it contributed some of my most trying moments.

CHAPTER 8

MANY OF THE NATIVES on Lubang had worked on Corregidor for American army men during the prewar period, and Rita knew a number of the inhabitants, so we were welcomed with the proverbial open arms. A young Spaniard, Jose Ramos—I called him Joe—was the big gun on the island, and the natives took us to his mountain retreat as soon as they learned I was an American army officer.

Joe had been a government-paid superintendent of construction on the island. There had been some military and emplacement projects under way with native labor, and this Spaniard had attained the position of high and mighty potentate through his disbursement of government funds. If some of our politicians had observed his methods, they would have grown green with envy. Anyway, Joe had a cozy mountain home from which you could see trucks moving on Corregidor on a pleasant day. Nearby was a clear pool in which Rita and I spent many pleasant hours. All this building had been done with government labor and government materials on government time and money; Joe even had his men throw up a bamboo home for Rita and me in the village, a short ways down the mountain and well protected from prying eyes on the sea.

The natives outfitted us with clothes and provided household furnishings and food, and I began living an idyllic life. I lounged around during the day, ate well, and thoroughly enjoyed myself. The natives were still untouched by the Jap-imposed civilization, and were happy. They were deeply religious and observed so many festivals and feast days that it seemed as though there was a picnic every day. I entered into the village life with a lot of enthusiasm, and I even tried the native dances, which resembled our square dances. I think the Filipinos enjoyed having me with them as much as I enjoyed being there. They had many laughs at my expense.

Rita kept house, and I spent a lot of time with Joe. He was a Filipino-born Spaniard and hated the Japs, although the Japs were friendly toward the Spaniards in the Philippines.

One day at dinner Rita told me that she was the niece of Emilio Aguinaldo, the ill-famed Benedict Arnold of the Philippines, who had returned to Tokyo with the Japanese and was even then cooperating with the Japs and living in luxury in Manila. When she mentioned his name her eyes glistened with rage. She was ashamed of the relationship, and said that if she ever got the chance, even though he was her uncle, she'd kill him. From the tone of her voice and the vigor with which she broke a chicken bone as she said it, I felt that Aguinaldo would be a dead cookie if Rita should ever meet him in an appropriate place.

To pass away time Joe and I began playing two-handed rummy, and then we switched to poker. The natives showed much interest, and we volunteered to teach them the game. It was a profitable enterprise. Joe and I'd sit by the hour in the shade of his porch with Corregidor in the distance, teaching from two to a half dozen Filipinos the art and finer points of the game. In the process of learning, the Filipinos didn't do very well and I won so many pesos I was afraid I would become one of the wealthiest men on the island. But they soon caught on to the game, being natural-born gamblers, and then the sessions on Joe's porch became tight affairs, and I lost some of my winnings. The only thing that would break up our game was the Sunday cockfights in the village. Everyone turned out, and betting was as wild as a college freshman on his first vacation.

The Japs had landed on the far end of the island, but the only ones we saw were patrols that occasionally visited the village, stayed for an hour, and then pushed on. We always had long-advance warning of their coming, and Rita and I hid in the woods.

Late one afternoon I was sitting on Joe's porch with my feet cocked up on a rail, looking out toward the sea, when the Spaniard broke the silence with a casual, "How'd you like to make a trip to Manila?"

I was so startled I nearly swallowed the cigarette I was smoking, and the legs of my chair hit the porch floor with a resounding clatter. I had heard via the bamboo tele-graph—a word-of-mouth communication system compa-rable to Bell's—that a number of Americans were still hiding in the city, and I knew further that General Wain-wright was living there in the University Club Apartments.

Although I was happy on Lubang, I had never given up hope of reaching Australia. In fact, I had been thinking about trying to contact some of the Americans in Manila, and perhaps even see General Wainwright and take a message from him to General MacArthur and our forces in the south. That is why I was so surprised when Joe broached the very subject that had been occupying my mind.

Joe departed that night to see his mother and sister in Manila, and three days later he returned with a pass for me under the name Ramon Gausa. He told me that when he applied for the pass, the Japs had asked my name after first making certain that I was Spanish. Joe had completely forgotten about a phony name, and said "Damon."

"Ramon?" inquired the Jap clerk.

"Yes," Joe stuttered, "Ramon Gausa."

There was to be much more double-talk before the trip was completed.

I was suitably outfitted with a white sharkskin suit provided by a native merchant and with a wide-brimmed straw hat characteristic of the Spaniards in the area. I let my mustache grow till it could be curled, and my sideburns grew two inches longer than they'd ever been in my life. I could speak Spanish but not with the Filipino accent, so Joe and I practiced. That is, I'd strut up and down his porch bowing and saying "Sí, señor!" with a flourish of my arm. We decided that I'd better stick to three words: "Sí, señor," and "no."

Rita was doubtful about the wisdom of my decision to enter Jap-infested Manila, but she was down to the boat to wave good-bye when, early in the morning, we shoved off for the mainland. Joe was big and ruddy and looked less like a Spaniard than I, so I wasn't too worried about being detected in the crowded city.

We docked at Batangas where we were to catch a bus for Manila, and there we encountered our first Jap sentries. We showed our passes and grinned condescendingly at the bastards, and after one looked at them an inordinately long time he raised his head and said happily, as if he'd just figured the pass out, "Speen, no?" meaning, "Spanish, yes?"

We nodded from the hips and bared our teeth in Jap-like smiles. He returned the pass, we exchanged another bow and walked on. Our credentials were examined several more times before we reached Manila about nightfall. We went immediately to Joe's home and spent the night there with his mother and sisters.

The next morning—it was late in June—we arose early and walked toward the Escolata, or main business district. The city was infested with uniformed Japs, and we bowed to all of them and stepped sideways to let them pass. Sometimes we'd salute them with "Buenos días, Señor," or "Mabuhay Nippon," which in Filipino meant "Long live Japan."

We went into several stores, but could buy nothing because we had none of the Jap money that was now being circulated in the city. Nobody seemed very happy. On one street we saw several naked Japs washing beside a hydrant in the street. The ladies who had to walk past modestly turned their heads. A couple of Japs stopped us, holding their bayoneted guns menacingly and asked in no uncertain terms if we were Americans.

We pretended we didn't understand English very well, shrugged our shoulders, and were absolutely the dumbest Spaniards the Japs would ever see. We got away with the hoax and worked our way to the University Club Apartments where General Wainwright was held prisoner. A cordon of guards were patrolling the area and we tried to appear nonchalant. We sauntered into the lobby and reached the stairs when a Jap waved a gun in our direction and we left without offering any argument. By this time I was wishing I was back on Lubang. It was simply impossible to contact the general. A Filipino girl who went to high school with Joe and was working in the hotel as a secretary for the Japs later told us that they even stationed a guard in the general's room at all times. She kept us informed about many other things, too.

We continued strolling through the streets, encountering the familiar difficulties. I laughed at the new names the Japs had given the streets; even Dewey Boulevard had been renamed for some Jap hero. Many of the old hot spots were closed but that night we went to a recently opened, Jap-operated nightclub. Joe knew a fancy hostess at the club and was anxious to see her, so I tagged along.

The girl was pretty all right, and decked out in a glittering gold, low-cut evening gown. I asked how she liked working for the Japs, being a Filipino. She answered that it was a job and, "What else can I do?"

We had been there a half hour and ordered a couple of rounds, and Rosita was describing the changes in the city. A Nip colonel and his aide, a captain, entered the club and took a seat three tables away facing us. They glanced our way often, and I wondered if they suspected anything. Rosita said she didn't think so, that they were frequent customers, and that the colonel had taken a liking to her.

I saw the colonel lean over and tell the captain something, out of the corner of my eye, and the aide sauntered over to our table, and very politely and in perfect English asked if we would join the colonel for a drink. The colonel bowed and smiled to accentuate his man's invitation. If I hadn't been so frightened I might have answered in English and queered our game, but my mouth suddenly became dry and I couldn't speak. However, with complete control and just the right amount of nonchalance Rosita said in Spanish the equivalent of "No, thank you."

But the captain was a persistent cuss, and asked with a good-neighbor smile if the colonel could join us and buy a drink. The girl could hardly refuse, so a waiter brought chairs and the colonel and captain sat down, the captain at my left. The colonel picked up the conversation in fluent Spanish and ordered drinks all around. It had been a long time since I was so scared. My knees were actually rattling.

I couldn't speak Spanish well enough to bandy words with these educated Japanese, so Rosita and Joe did most of the talking. I drank. In fact, I drank more than any of the others and whenever I was asked a question I put a glass to my mouth and turned the other way. I figured that my only way out was to at least pretend that I was drunk, and I put on a good show. The colonel laughed at me and dismissed me as a soak, no doubt. The conversation carefully avoided the Jap-Filipino issue. The colonel was trying to date Rosita, and she was skillfully parrying his leading questions and taking very good care of herself.

Whenever it looked as though they were waiting for an answer from me, I looked as silly as I could and smiled. After a while they ignored me, and I dropped my head on my chest and pretended to sleep, but I couldn't have fallen asleep in a feather bed. The Japs sat with us for a couple of hours, long enough so that I nearly had the D.T.'s before the party broke up. The colonel insisted that he take Joe and me home "since we were such gay and delightful caballeros," and once more my heart jumped out of its normal resting place. I could see myself going on the equivalent of a "Chicago ride."

The captain took my arm to help me and I probably couldn't have walked, drunk or sober, without his help because I was so frightened my legs wouldn't function properly. I knew where I wanted to put them, but somehow or other they just wouldn't fall into place. It all added to the realism of my drunk act. When we reached the canopied entrance a Jap staff car was waiting, and a soldier opened the door smartly, and three of us piled into the rear seat while the colonel rode in front. I returned to sleep, or shut my eyes, as soon as the car started, and there was little conversation on the way to Joe's place. When we stopped, the captain helped Joe get me out of the car, and both he and the colonel bid us a friendly good night and even I recovered sufficiently to say, "Long Live Japan!" "Viva Japan!"

Joe assisted me inside the house, and I went right to my room, got my few personal belongings together, and in an hour I was on my way out of the city toward Batangas and my boat. Joe was remaining in Manila but I had had enough.

CHAPTER 9

MOST OF THE NIGHT was spent in the little boat, and when the sun shot above the mainland mountains and glistened off the white, curving wave tops I was only a mile from my landing place on Lubang. The island looked so green and fresh in the early morning sunlight that I was happy to be alive. I was especially appreciative of nature's wonders that morning. It was the reverse of a hangover.

I had all I could do to beach the boat safely in the fast surf; when I stepped nimbly out on the beach I was face-to-face with Rita, but a Rita I had never seen before. She was barefoot and clad in a wraparound piece of gaudy cotton cloth. Her hair hung loosely below her waist, and I wondered if I had stumbled onto a Dorothy Lamour set.

She was watching for my reaction, I knew, and although I actually was taken aback at what had been "coming off" in the few days I was away, I told Rita that she looked comfortable anyway. She said that she'd tried the sarong outfit and liked it, so . . . You can't argue with a woman in the matter of dress. Rita thought I might be back that morning, so had come down to meet me. Nothing of importance had taken place during my absence, but a native had brought in the information that another American officer was being harbored in a neighboring island; I sent the man back with a note addressed to the officer, if he could find him.

The natives, all of whom knew that I had been to Manila, were anxious to hear about my trip, and they roared with delight, some even doubling up with laughter, when I related how the Jap captain had helped me in and out of his car. I was rather pleased when I saw how the Filipinos reacted to the story, although I had seen nothing humorous in the situation when the Jap colonel was peering at me and shaking his head in pity for a confirmed drunkard.

I waited several weeks for an answer to the message I had sent the reported American officer, and then came word via the bamboo telegraph that the Japs were readying a force to take over the island. It was time to act so I hurriedly abandoned the pleasant village life, bid Rita good-bye for a while, and with a native boy set out in the boat for an island three days distant where I had been told an American colonel was living.

The boy left me at the first village we encountered on the island, and I continued along the coast looking for the landmarks that were to guide me to the colonel. I was looking for the mouth of a river, but darkness fell and I still hadn't found it, so I beached the boat and plodded along the beach with a flashlight. The river cut into the ocean at a sharp angle, which made it difficult to find, but I returned to the boat and after about an hour I was nosing my craft carefully up the well-hidden stream. It was deep enough so that schooners sailed as far as the colonel's town. I climbed aboard a boat that was resting forlornly on the bottom and slept till daylight. Once more I started slowly up the stream, and about noon I reached the village. I inquired of a cluster of natives where I might find Colonel Wells, since that name had been given me, and they pointed to a bamboo hut.

A white man on the porch fanning himself with a leaf watched my progress from the river bank. A score of natives followed at my heels, and the ever-present dogs bounded ahead along the sun-baked road. I placed one foot on the bottom step of the porch and said, "I'm Lieutenant Gause, an American army officer."

The man stood, extended his hand, and answered, "My name is Sta-a-a, Wells, I'm glad to see you."

Although he said he was glad to see me, he didn't act it. His hesitation when he mentioned his name should have aroused my suspicion then, but I was so delighted to find another white man that I overlooked it—until later.

Wells was about 45 years old, and had been living in the Philippines for many years. When I returned to the States I learned that he was a graduate of Yale University and had traveled extensively through Europe. He was ill with fever when I arrived and was troubled with a sore on the calf of his leg. It was festering and wouldn't heal, forcing him to limp, dragging the sore leg up to the other with each step.

The colonel told me any number of fantastic stories during the first few days I was with him, and I wondered if it was the fever or if he was a little off the beam because of his lonely existence. For instance, he said that he was connected with American naval intelligence, and since he had also been an Army colonel that I could talk freely with him. I told him of my hopes of reaching Australia but volunteered no additional information.

The colonel found me a place to sleep in his house and I ate with him about two weeks. One day he asked me, since he still was not strong, if I'd go to a boat he had moored in the river and get some important hidden papers and passports. I was certainly surprised to see a sleek two-masted schooner, completely outfitted and ready to sail at a moment's notice. I had to use a chisel to pry up the deck boards. On the way back to the house with the papers I began to wonder about the colonel. He was intensely interested in news from the European theater and often spoke encouragingly about Germany and the things the Germans were fighting for. I asked a few questions of the natives, but all they knew was that he had sailed up the river with a native girl with whom he was living.

The Fourth of July arrived while I was at Colonel Wells's. The big American holiday was always suitably observed in the Philippines, but the natives were a bit apprehensive on this Fourth because the area was filled with Japs who were on the lookout for any patriotic displays. A Filipino boy on Lubang had given me an American flag he had taken from Corregidor after the fortress was surrendered, and I had hidden it on my boat. I remembered it on the Fourth, however, and after breaking it out and unwrapping it, the colonel and I ran it to the top of a coconut palm in the center of the village.

There was a nice breeze, and the flag billowed out as prettily as anything I had ever seen. In about an hour natives began pouring into the village from surrounding towns, and I was informed that we were to have a Fourth of July observance, Japs or no Japs. After a noon meal that was really a festive occasion everybody, men, women, children—even the dogs—crowded around the tree that served as a flagstaff and, after I started it, their voices rose in a fervent salute to the flag. Then in my jungle falsetto and at too high a pitch, I sang a few words of "The Star-Spangled Banner," and the guitars and stringed instruments that had been playing for the dinner picked up the tune. In a flash every Filipino crowded into the square was lustily singing our national anthem. Some sang in English and some in Tagalog, but they all knew the words and even sang two choruses. When the last words died away there was the usual hush that follows the song, and then they broke away in groups and returned to their work. Their Fourth of July celebration was over and I hauled in the flag and stored it back in the boat.

That night as I sat on the colonel's porch and smoked, slapping at mosquitoes, the words "I pledge allegiance to the flag of the United States of America"—as spoken by these humble Filipinos—rang in my ears. There was no worry about fifth columnists among them. Like their countrymen throughout the islands they were intensely loyal to the Americans. I wouldn't be writing this if they hadn't been. As I mused to myself I thought how extraordinary was this patriotic spirit after we had been humiliated and driven out of their country.

I rocked back and forth, and the squeak of my chair rivaled the groans that arose from the porch flooring. Why couldn't I remain in the Philippines until after the war? In the past two months I had escaped detection and lived comfortably, and if I did push off for Australia the chances were 10 to 1 that I wouldn't get there. This was the first time I gave serious consideration to an idea I had been struggling with and banishing for weeks.

A few days after the Fourth I was sitting on the bank of the river, idly tossing pebbles at floating coconuts and logs, when I saw a white man wading upstream on the opposite bank, occasionally ducking his head beneath low branches. I returned to Wells's hut, always keeping the newcomer within sight. I saw him bargain with a native to row him across the river. When he stepped out on the beach I watched him speak to a group of natives and they pointed toward our house.

Just before he reached our steps I walked out to meet him, and after introducing ourselves, we clapped each other on the arms and shoulders and fairly jumped with joy. He was Captain William Lloyd Osborne, American commander of a Filipino infantry company, who had escaped from Bataan and had been hiding in the jungles with a handful of his scouts. He had received my note sent by messenger weeks ago, and had seen Rita on Lubang and followed me to Colonel Wells.

I hustled the captain into the house to meet the colonel, talking excitedly all the time, visualizing a way of escape at last. But when the colonel arose from a couch in response to my call and faced the new arrival, I saw Osborne's face set, and he stepped back a pace and lifted his right hand to his hip, about where he would have carried a gun. The colonel smiled, however, and hospitably suggested that "we three live together as Americans all."

The undercover hostility that I sensed worried me and after supper I asked Osborne to walk down to the river with me. As soon as we were out of earshot of the house, the captain hurriedly explained that Wells was not an American soldier but a reported German alien, whom he himself had arrested in Batangas a few days before the outbreak of war. Wells had murdered his guard, however, and slipped past the cordon of police and soldiers who were dispatched to intercept him.

The news was quite a shock to me, but after discussing the pros and cons we decided that we had no other place to go that night, so we returned to the hut. I told Osborne about the colonel's schooner, and we both saw in it a possible means of escape.

I noticed a distinct change in the colonel's manner toward me during the next few days, although neither the captain nor myself I ever mentioned that we knew his past record. The third day after Osborne arrived—we had been laying plans all this time—I asked the colonel if he had a rifle, that I'd like to hunt some fresh meat for our table. He said he never kept weapons of any kind, but I doubted that statement after hearing from Osborne how handy he had been with a revolver when he killed the Filipino guard.

That same night I was lying on the bamboo floor in my room; Osborne was breathing deeply in the far corner. I was hot, the mosquitoes were bothering me, and sleep had been difficult the last few nights because I was so excited about our chances of escape. The wind was sighing through the cracks in the bamboo wall and moving the netting above my face very gently—when my eye was attracted by a movement in the far and dark corner near the door.

I remained motionless, but every sense sprang to the alert as I watched closely. For perhaps thirty seconds there was no further movement, and then a figure glided silently out of the shadows and was silhouetted in the window. It was Colonel Wells, and he was holding a revolver in his right hand. His injured leg made a soft scraping noise as he drew it up to his good leg and took step after step directly toward me. Osborne slept blissfully in the other corner.

He intended to kill me, I was sure, and then finish Osborne before the latter could move into action. He stopped about six inches from my body. I had my eye on the gun, waiting for him to aim it, and I noticed his fingers clench and unclench around the handle. Without further waiting I threw myself at his legs, tackle fashion, and knocked him roughly to the floor. I made a lunge for his right hand and clamped his wrist with my left hand, squeezing as hard as I could. With my right, I worked to pry his revolver loose from his iron like fingers.

We rolled across the floor, knocking over a chair. With a quick move the colonel twisted the gun down by his side, but in the next instant I tore it from his grasp and it went off. His body slumped down on top of me, but I pushed it off and scrambled to my feet holding the gun.

Osborne was jumping with excitement. The noise of the scuffle had awakened him, but in the dark he didn't know who I was fighting with or even which of the struggling men was me. In few words I explained what had happened. The colonel's woman appeared at the door with a candle, the only light in the house. She displayed no emotion on seeing Wells lying motionless on the floor. Natives awakened by the shot were running, shouting, to the house, so Osborne and I hightailed out the front door and ran for my boat. In minutes we were floating with the current, and then two paddles were lifting the boat forward.

I don't believe Wells was killed by the bullet. He was shot in the stomach, since we were both struggling for the weapon near his hip, but he was badly wounded. Since he was sick, I could have overpowered him easily once I obtained the gun, but I didn't get full control of the weapon until after it discharged. I now had a pistol at any rate. I later discovered that the Army Intelligence Department was interested to learn of "Colonel Wells's" whereabouts and possible end. For years he had been in the employ of the Nazi government in the Philippines and was probably in thick with the Japs, as well. But until the last night he had treated me with courtesy.

On our way back to Lubang, Captain Osborne and I decided that it'd be "Australia or bust." All question or doubt had vanished from my mind. The burning desire to reach Australia, my forces, and my loved ones, which had burned before and then died down, was blazing again. I was a bit apprehensive about returning to Lubang because, by this time, I had come to care for Rita more than I should have, under the circumstances, and I asked myself if I would have strength enough to leave her there alone after all that she had done for me. We had also heard by the usually reliable bamboo telegraph that the Japs had come to the island and were in complete control. We cautiously maneuvered into a deserted cove, however, and when we learned that the Japs had departed leaving a Filipino-appointed governor in charge we made our way at once to my Filipino "hometown."

Rita had been ill with the fever, as were many of the

natives, and her hatred of the Japs had been trebled, if that could be possible. The Nips had stripped the island of quinine, rice, chickens, pigs—all kinds of food—and fishing boats; but the loss of quinine with which they combated fever was the greatest loss. These people who had been so gay and carefree a month ago had felt the heavy and cruel hand of the oppressor and were visibly affected.

I heard of a boat that had been confiscated by the Japs, but was lying unused on a nearby isle, which was harboring some soldiers. I contacted the Filipino owner, a man named Tividad, and he agreed to help Osborne and me steal the craft, a 20-foot, native-built motor skiff. We told him about our plans, and Tividad said he believed we could make Australia in about four months. He, and Rita of course, were the only persons on the island who believed that we would ever see our destination.

The natives knew I was preparing to leave, and they did their utmost to make my remaining few days pleasant. One even brought me an old *National Geographic* map of Oceania that was of inestimable value to us on the voyage. I had long talks with the natives, learning the best routes, the topography of the islands we should pass, and the possible dangers we would encounter. Important supplies for the trip were gathered, a few here and a few there, until nothing remained between us and Australia—I foolishly believed—except a boat trip.

Tividad was a spunky fellow. He sailed with us to the island and pointed out the boat lying above the water line. It wasn't much to look at but it was a luxury liner to us. When high tide came we struggled to shove it off the beach. It wouldn't budge out of its sandy bed. Then a half dozen Filipinos strolled down the beach to see what was taking place and volunteered to help us. One of the men had been the mechanic and operator of the boat's cranky little engine. At first he thought we were Japs and stood and watched in scornful silence, but when he found out that we were American army officers, he gladly pitched in and told us all he knew about the boat and engine.

A dozen small boats from Lubang then arrived and hauled alongside. They were carrying supplies that they had been hoarding, but which they gave to us unselfishly when they heard we were determined to sail for a faraway land called "Australia." Quickly and silently the natives carried on the job of transferring the foodstuffs, fruit, and other things that they knew we must have to make such a long trip. Tividad's mechanic worked feverishly with the rusted and balky motor, and it was soon sputtering reluctantly. Tividad tossed a pile of flour sacks into the boat and told us where we could find a man to help us sew them into a crude sail and get a mast. All the time these preparations were in progress, Rita hovered around the boat like a small boy looking forward to a long trip during his summer vacation.

Just before dawn we were ready to shove-off. We said thanks, and meant it, to Tividad and his men and to our Filipino friends, who were standing in their beached boats or knee-deep in water waiting for us to weigh anchor. They were all my friends. Yes, every man, woman, and child. I had lived with them for over two months, and as they watched intently in the grayness of dawn I felt a personal duty to every one of them. It was even more difficult for me to say "good-bye" to Rita and her kinsmen than I had anticipated, but I knew it had to be done.

Then there was Rita standing on the bow waving 'bye to her friends and assuring them that we would make it. I finally mustered up enough courage to tell her that she couldn't go. She broke down, and I saw her cry for the first time during our strange acquaintance. When I handed her over the rail to a Filipino boy, I felt as if I had handed him my right arm. However, she regained her composure quickly, and I shall never forget how she looked that morning in the early morning light, standing knee deep in the surf, with her long dark hair hanging to her waist, bravely waving good-bye with the tears slipping slowly down her cheeks. She embodied all the qualities of a mythical Philippine goddess of loyalty, love, and liberty.

CHAPTER 10

OUR ARK BY DAYLIGHT was a sorry sight. It was poorly equipped, leaked, needed sail, and the motor was a hit-or-miss affair, mostly miss. In midmorning we put in at a quiet cove where nestled a native village described by Tividad. We remained there two days and received all kinds of Filipino help to sew sails, erect a mast, patch and scrape the boat, and store it with some badly needed supplies. I worked on the diesel motor, making some experiments that the mechanic had said would help. Before we left, Osborne and I filled a used beer bottle with water and christened the ship *Ruth-Lee,* for our wives.

Captain Osborne was my army superior and therefore entitled to give orders, which I must obey, but before shoving off we agreed that while on the boat I should be boss. Osborne admitted that he knew nothing about sailing, and although my knowledge of boats had been gleaned since Rita and I left the mainland, I figured I could handle the ship. Osborne called me "Skipper" on the boat. I called him "Mate." Ashore, I called him "Captain"; he called me "anything."

The afternoon we moved out of the cove I was full of

confidence that we'd cover the 3,200 miles across the Jap-infested and hazardous seas to Australia. Our ship looked pretty good, but an hour later, and many times thereafter, I decided I'd been overly optimistic.

Filipino friends had informed us that large supplies of kerosene, something we needed badly if we were to operate the motor, were stored on a small and rocky lighthouse island—Capra—near the channel leading to Manila Bay. We were headed for the lighthouse when a wild rain and thunderstorm broke just before nightfall. The little craft pitched and tossed, but the motor kept running, and when the welcoming lighthouse window poked up over the crest of the towering waves we steered directly toward it.

There was no dock, so we beached the boat on the leeward side of the rocky isle, a ticklish proposition in the storm and wind. We sneaked toward the base of the lighthouse tower where lights flickered from two slit windows about six feet above the ground. The wind was howling, and the beating rain and occasional bursts of thunder made detection a slim possibility. I dragged a log across the slippery rocks, placed it beneath the window and clambered up to carefully peek through the rain-spattered pane.

A lone Jap, buck teeth and all, with a revolver strapped to his side, was sitting alone reading. Osborne and I conferred, and then he went to the door at the front of the building and rapped, while I unlimbered the revolver I had taken from the colonel and held it in readiness between the bars that guarded the window. At the first rap the Jap put down his book and unconcernedly ap-

Rocky Gause in front of the Joe DiMaggio Cafe in San Francisco, California, shortly before leaving for the Philippine Islands in late October 1941.

Jesycene Gause shown with her children *(left to right)*:
Millie, John, Audrey, Rocky, and Wilson.

Rocky was an active
child who loved animals.

Rocky *(kneeling at left)* as a teenager,
with some of his many friends.

Rocky and friend shown working
for Texaco Oil Company
in South America.

Ruth L. Gause, shown
in a 1943 photo.

Ruth and Rocky at Hunter Field in
Savannah, Georgia, prior to their
marriage on October 11, 1941.
Rocky left the United States on the
USS *Coolidge* on November 1 with
the 27th Bombardment Group
(Light) as a dive-bomber pilot whose
next duty station would be the
Philippine Islands.

British compass similar to the one which was given to Rocky
and Capt. Lloyd Osborne by a leper on Culion Island
in the Philippines. The small hand-held compass was
their only navigational instrument.

Rocky's journal.

"Three American Marine escapees captured on Corregidor, escaped on Palawan Island. Left to right, George Davis, Sid Wright, and Buddy Henderson. These Marines helped refit our boat. They elected to stay on Palawan to try to free other prisoners. It was on this island that Miss Nancy Howland from Indiana, a Methodist missionary, gave us a box camera and several rolls of film with which the pictures were taken. September 5, 1942. DJG"

"Me at the helm of the *Ruth-Lee* in the Makassar Strait.
September 15, 1942. DJG"

"A typical native village on the wild jungle-laden western coast of Celebes Island.
September 20, 1942. DJG"

"A Moro schoolmaster and his son on the small island of Cagayan in the southern
Philippine Islands. September 10, 1942. DJG"

"A typical native hut on the beautiful mountainous island of Sumba. All the natives shown here live in the hut in the background. Taken by Captain Osborne. October 1, 1942. DJG"

"Native inhabitants of a village on the Japanese-held island of Sumba.
October 1, 1942. DJG"

"Looking astern on the *Ruth-Lee* on the northern coast of Australia. October 4, 1942. DJG"

"Captain Lloyd Osborne and me on the last day of our escape from the Philippine Islands. Taken October 11, 1942 by our Aussie guide. October 11, 1942. DJG"

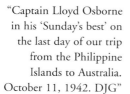

"Captain Lloyd Osborne in his 'Sunday's best' on the last day of our trip from the Philippine Islands to Australia. October 11, 1942. DJG"

Rocky Gause and Lloyd Osborne shown with their escape boat, *Empress of Mindoro*, which they renamed and christened *Ruth-Lee* after their wives.

"Captain Osborne and me standing as free men on Australian soil on October 13, 1942. 'Old Glory' is proudly held between us. On this day with a simple statement we closed our ship's log that we had maintained: 'We close this log with immense rejoicing.' October 13, 1942. DJG"

"Major Craig, an Australian officer, Osborne, and myself
at Wyndham, Australia. A homemade Japanese flag around
Captain Osborne's waist helped us trick the Japanese
on many occasions. October 13, 1942. DJG"

After 159 days, Rocky couldn't wait to get a shave and a haircut.

Rocky Gause at a reception in his honor at Winder, Georgia, in November 1942 just after returning home from his lengthy escape. *Left to right:* Rocky's wife, Ruth; his father, D.A.; Rocky; his mother, Jesycene; and Winder, Georgia, Mayor H. T. Flanigan.

Senator Richard Russell, Georgia's long-standing U.S. senator, shown introducing Captain Gause after his escape from the Philippines. *From left to right:* Gause's sisters, Millie and Audrey; his parents, Duff and Jesycene; and Rocky with his wife, Ruth, behind him.

Rocky and Ruth attending an Armistice Day reception in the Ansley Hotel in Atlanta, Georgia, in early 1943.

Rocky Gause as command-
ing officer of the 324th
Fighter Group at the
Richmond Air Base in
1943. Men addressing
Captain Gause were
required to stand on the
homemade Japanese flag
that had been successfully
used to trick the enemy.
The American flag behind
him had been removed by
a native Filipino and
entrusted to Gause and
Osborne to bring to safety.

Rocky and his dog, Butch, after arriving home from the escape.

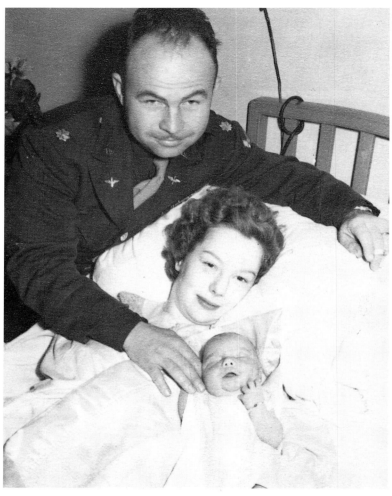

Rocky shown with Ruth and their young son, Damon Lance, on December 9, 1943, at St. Mary's Hospital in Athens, Georgia. This was the only time Rocky ever saw his son and the last time he saw his wife. He had been promoted to major on December 7, 1943—the date his only child was born.

Rocky with Colonel Lance Call, group commander of the 365th Fighter-Bomber Group while stationed at Richmond Air Base. Rocky's son, Damon Lance, was named after Rocky's commanding officer, who allowed Rocky to slip away to see his son before leaving for the European Theater on December 12, 1943.

Rocky in front of his P-47 Thunderbolt fighter plane at Richmond Air Base in 1943.

D. J. GAUSE

Rocky at Richmond Air Base in 1943.

Rocky at Richmond
Air Base in 1943.

Rocky Gause's grave marker at the
American Cambridge military cemetery
in Cambridge, England.

proached the door. He opened it a crack, and I plunged my gun through the glass pane, shouting at the top of my lungs yet saying nothing intelligible. At the same time my mate pushed through the door and grabbed the undecided Jap before he could even reach for his gun. I rejoined Osborne, and we tied our captive and tossed him in a closet. Now Osborne also had a gun. We were doing all right.

Four Filipino workers living in a rear room hadn't even heard the commotion, but when they saw us and took in the situation, they offered to help us load our boat with about fifty five-gallon cans of kerosene. Then they produced ammunition they had hidden in miscellaneous parts of the island, and when we last saw them they had filled another small boat with kerosene and were off in the direction of the mainland.

The lighthouse was thoroughly ransacked before we left, and we added to our stores much-needed rope, tea, coffee, sugar, and fruit. What we couldn't use we destroyed. Without bothering to eat we pushed the *Ruth-Lee* into deeper water and started the motor, hoping to put as much distance as possible between us and the island. It was impossible to tell, however, if we were making progress in the dark because I shot out the light before leaving. We just held a steady course and prayed.

The wind and rain that slashed down on our craft the rest of the night, and the turbulent seas that flowed in treacherous currents through the channels between the islands played havoc with the *Ruth-Lee*. Waves burst over the prow, adding to the water already in the boat from leaks in the hull. The island of Mindoro loomed up in front of us, black and huge in the leaden skies, and we nursed the boat into a deserted and quiet cove, both hidden and protected from the sea by a curving neck of land.

The first thing I did when the storm subsided was to construct a folding bunk out of bamboo. It was fastened against the wall of a crude cabin that covered the front of the *Ruth-Lee* so it could be folded back when not in use. The cabin protected perishable supplies and the engine, which like all of its kind gave off acrid fumes and noise. (Even though its racket was music to our ears, many times it made sleep virtually impossible.) The Filipinos had described a caulking material called apo made out of lime and coconut oil, and using that we patched up the holes and seams until the craft was more watertight than it had been for weeks.

A wild tribe of natives lived in the Mindoro mountains, we had been told, but the first few days we were there we saw nobody. Legend was that Spanish prisoners had fled into the interior during one of the invasions characteristic of the early Philippine history, and had bred the supposedly wild race. The fourth day of our labors on the island I had a suspicion that somebody was watching us. I spoke to Osborne about it, and while I was working on the boat, up to my knees in water, I'd glance up suddenly and see a branch or a bush move ever so slightly in the jungle growth along the shore. It was a nerve-racking experience. My revolver was on my belt, but I hitched it around where I could grab it in a hurry. We were sleeping on the boat, but that night when I was on watch I kept an extra-sharp lookout.

When the suspected figures did emerge from the jungle

on the following day, they had almost walked up to us before we noticed them. One was a very old man, ninety at least, and he was accompanied by two younger men. Remembering the wild tribe stories, I anticipated trouble, but the old man spoke Spanish fairly well and we made friends easily. They were of the much-talked-about lost tribe, all right, and though I asked many questions they were very reticent about their living habits. They had seen our boat in the cove from the mountains and had decided to investigate. That was all.

They watched us work for a few hours and then began helping us. We were scouring the five-gallon oil cans with sand and then boiling them in water, preparatory to refilling them with fresh water for our long journey. They took over this job and then helped us load fruit, and when we shoved off late in the day, they waved as enthusiastically as any of the other Filipinos we encountered. The trio had been clad only in Mahatma Gandhi shorts and as the *Ruth-Lee* nosed out of the seclusion of the bay, I wondered if, after all, they hadn't found the secret of a happy and peaceful life. They were certainly isolationists.

A dozen miles further around Mindoro (our boat was cutting through the sea nicely now), a very small native village appeared. There were perhaps a dozen huts, so we put in and found the natives friendly and as pro-American as the Brooklynites are pro-Dodger. Several more days were spent bartering for supplies. Using money "borrowed" at the lighthouse, we purchased rice, and I resurrected a gun and went into the jungle one day with two natives and shot a carabao—the Philippine counterpart of a steer—and a wild pig. The natives dressed the meat and applied their own kind of preservative, and that, too, was stored on the boat. These Filipinos, when they heard that our little boat was to sail as far as Australia—a remote and fantastic place to them—shook their heads at the folly of the Americanos. Nevertheless, they pitched in with vigor to fit the *Ruth-Lee* and when we got ready to move along with the big trip, I was confident that our boat was as seaworthy as it would ever be—that's what I thought then, anyway.

We had an American flag on the boat, the one that came from Corregidor, which I used at Colonel Wells's, a Filipino flag from Bataan, and a Japanese flag that I made with materials taken from the lighthouse. I had also prepared a white flag that was sort of a precautionary measure to show that we were uninterested. The other flags, of course, were to be unfurled as the occasion demanded, since we would be sailing through enemy water all of the way.

As we drew away from the little native village, however, the American flag was waving defiantly, and the villagers lined the shore and their naked children ran excitedly up and down the beach waving their hands and cheering. With the send-off we were accorded, you might have believed that the *Ruth-Lee* was the pride of the American Pacific fleet instead of a patched-up derelict of questionable seaworthiness.

It was mid-August when we left Mindoro, and since at last we were Australia-bound I started to keep a log in a little book I had put together on Lubang, in which I had written haphazardly up to this time. My first entry in the log was:

August 20, 1942

Port of departure	Santa Cruz, Mindoro, P.I.
Boat's Name	*Ruth-Lee*
Captain	Damon J. Gause
Mate and Crew	William L. Osborne
Trip No.	No. 1—South
Port of destination	Port Darwin, Australia
Time of sailing	6:00 P.M. O.W.T.
"Bon voyage"	

D. J. Gause
Captain

Osborne and I now became very nautical. He called me Skipper all the time and I referred to him as mate. But that bit of subterfuge didn't fool our gastric juices. We were in the open sea about an hour, and the *Ruth-Lee* was pitching like a bronco when I began to feel very weak, especially in the vicinity of my stomach. When my mate—who was looking even more pale than usual—made a dive for the side of the boat, that was enough for me. Locating a comfortable spot on the other side of the boat, I, too, fed the fishes. We were saving food for the next two days, but it was most distressing, mentally and physically. While I held the tiller, Osborne occupied his side of the rail, and when he recovered sufficiently so that he could stagger back to the tiller, I looked for my reflection in the water. But after two days in the China Sea, our stomachs returned to their

normal positions, and we had no more seasickness the remainder of the voyage.

Osborne handled the cooking and the commissary duties while my job was to oversee the sails and operation of
the boat. We decided to split the night into two shifts,
depending on the weather or the situation at hand, and of
course in bad weather we were both on deck.

The first night out of Mindoro, and this added to the
bodily discomfort caused by seasickness, a Japanese ship
overtook us. It was a bright tropical night with millions
of stars, and when our eyes became accustomed to the
dark it was fairly easy to see. I thought, nevertheless, that
being sick was making me see a dark shadow a few hundred yards away. When a light began flashing from that
shadow, however, I watched pop-eyed. The Japs were sig-
naling by blinker light and they repeated the signals after
a pause. I collected my thoughts and watched closely. It
was the international Morse code, I was sure, but it was
too rapid for me, so I fished our flashlight out of a tool
kit and was holding it at shoulder level, still undecided
what to answer. The boat had obviously slowed, waiting
for a reply.

I knew only two Japanese words and purging my mind
to recall the code, I flashed "Bansai Nippon" (Long live
Japan). For seconds there was no answer from the boat that
could only have been a transport, so I spelled out the words
"Bansai Nippon" once more and prayed that the letters
were right. After what seemed like an intolerably long time
the Jap blinker went into action again, and we got the
"Proceed" signal. I proceeded to my customary rail posi-

tion, and was happy to be sick without a boatload of Japs watching.

We were recovering our health, and I had decided that you must have to be awfully sick to die, when the temperamental diesel motor chugged convulsively a few times and stopped dead. We had named her the "Little Swede" but now we added a few more names. Try as I could—I even talked to the balky thing—I couldn't get it started. Then I cursed it; I even beat it with a wrench, but still it wouldn't start. The sail was carrying us along at about a slow swimmer's pace. The motor needed some major repairs, I saw, so Osborne and I held a council of war. It wasn't in Casablanca, but it was mighty important.

When I had been puttering around Wells's boat I discovered an old pilot's chart of the islands and immediately appropriated it. We now spread this and our *National Geographic* map of the Far East on the deckhouse top and tried to ascertain our position. We had no instruments, but by tracing our course on the map from island to island, we were able to keep pretty good track of our location. According to our map, and if our previous calculations were correct, the island of Busuanga was dead ahead. The island was famous, or infamous, because the world's largest leper colony was situated in the town of Culion.

We were making little progress in the heavy seas and light wind, so we decided to try and make Culion Island. I knew there were some American doctors there, but I did not know the political situation, or whether the place was in Japanese control. I believed, though, that the Japs would stay as far removed from the lepers as they could.

Culion was on one side of Coron Bay, and facing it across the water was a large Japanese garrison controlling the operation of one of the largest base-metal mines in the Far East. We made a little better time when we gained the protection of Coron Bay, but we still kept a sharp lookout toward the garrison side of the bay. Danger lay there, we were sure, but what was in store for us at Culion was still uncertain.

The leper city was an inviting little place, except for the disease connected with it. Smart white houses and business structures, resembling tombstones from the distance, dominated by a large hospital building stuck up from the terraced hillside. I didn't think of that resemblance then, and that was fortunate because I was leery as it was about bouncing into a leper colony.

A half mile from the pier that jutted out into the water a raft approached our boat with a man and woman paddling. I was more interested in the city—and the Jap garrison—than the little raft, but from about twenty-five yards the man shouted and asked if we had any sugar to sell. They stopped paddling to listen for an answer, and when none came they dipped their paddles energetically once more and were soon keeping pace with our lumbering scow and jockeying into position so they could come aboard.

I had never seen a leper, and I watched them unconcernedly for perhaps a minute before it dawned on me that the ugly, bluish bumps on their faces and all over their bodies and the nauseating stench were the physical signs of the dread disease. I jumped off my seat and almost skidded on my back on the wet decking. "Go away, we have nothing to sell!" I commanded in the most persuasive Tagalog I could muster. At the same time I motioned energetically with my arms to emphasize what I had said.

The couple persisted in coming aboard, and drew so close that I could see that both had lost parts of several fingers at the joints, signifying that they were in the last stages of the disease. I could see myself with the sign "Leper" hanging around my neck. At last we made our threats so plain that they paddled back to shore and I was much relieved.

When we tied up at the wharf, I left Osborne in charge of the boat while I climbed up on the pier and inquired of the native stevedores where I could locate the governor of the island. I could see that these men were not lepers, so I felt a little better as I walked toward the single-story stucco structure that was pointed out as the governor's office. I was wearing only my regular pair of shorts, and had been burned almost black by the sun. My hair was as long as was my beard, and my revolver hung from my belt. I was certainly going to make quite an impression on the governor, I thought, but I wondered whether it would be favorable.

The door opened directly into the governor's office. A middle-aged, bespectacled man clad in a white suit and flanked by two armed Filipino guards sat behind a mahogany desk writing. My entrance was worthy of the most popular debutante into a grand ballroom. The governor glared at me, straightening up in his chair. I expected any minute that the guards would be ordered to "Seize that man!" as they do in adventure stories, but I walked over toward him with my hand outstretched, and if it was shaking as much as my knees it must have been waving.

"I am an American army officer," I began, and his frigid glance chilled the stifling room as he arose to accept my hand. "I sailed here in a boat with another officer who's waiting on the beach and we are badly in need of supplies."

When he heard I was an American I could see that the balance had swung in our favor. He said he would help us, although he had been placed in charge of the island by the Japs across the bay. At his suggestion we moved the boat down the coast a ways and up a creek, where we anchored it in a position where we could work on it. Then my mate and I traversed the half mile back to Culion, and Dr. Nolasco, the governor, introduced us to Dr. Wade, an American who had devoted most of his life to the leper colony; Dr. Wade in turn introduced us to Dr. Hanks and his wife, Americans also who were working among the lepers. All were interned by the Japs under the control of Dr. Nolasco.

The Americans were genuinely delighted to see us and we received an invitation to dinner that night. I sat down at the table—it was actually covered with a linen tablecloth—without shoes or shirt, but I enjoyed the civilized meal and we all had a great talk, mostly discussing the war and the States. After dinner, Dr. Hanks broke out his last bottle of Scotch and his last box of cigars and we sat and drank and smoked until late.

The next morning we went to work on our boat in earnest. The governor assigned a mechanic to the craft hoping to repair the engine in a couple of hours and get us on our merry way. But it was not as easy as all that. The engine was badly worn, but the mechanic was a first-class man and with tools from the colony shop he manufactured a gasket out of asbestos and repaired several other damaged parts. When we finally did sail, the boat was in fair shape once more, thanks largely to his ingenuity.

The propeller shaft needed straightening so that was another job we undertook, and the holes and seams were made as watertight as possible. Each noon the American women sent a hot lunch down to us by Mrs. Hanks's two sons, and whenever we left the boat the boys stayed and looked after it. Mrs. Hanks also gave us each a sweater she had been knitting for the Filipino army before war broke out. They were midriff style on Osborne and myself because they were intended for little Filipinos, but they were clothes. Each afternoon we joined the island social set and had tea at the home of one of the doctors, and every night we had dinner with one of the American families.

The oil supply that operated the island electric power system was running low so the power plant was only in use between seven and eight o'clock each night, primarily so that the Culion residents could hear the world news broadcasts. Work on the boat, such as welding and cutting, that had to be done with the use of electricity was also put off till the seven-to-eight period when we hustled to finish the job. I suppose those people still huddle around their radios each night at that hour, straining their ears for hopeful news about the war.

The doctors convinced us that leprosy was not as easy to contract as people believed. They said that there had been only one known case of contraction on the island, but that constant association with people who had the malady or with their personal belongings might pass on the sickness.

A high wire fence divided Culion, with about 500 non-lepers living on one side—the side where we spent our time—and possibly 5,000 lepers living on the other. Dr. Wade had a compass at the hospital he wanted to give us. It was a serious need, so one afternoon I bumped my nerve up and crossed the barrier to the leper side. I walked in the middle of the street toward the hospital, carefully avoiding the lepers who sat on their doorsteps and lined the streets. They were in all stages of the disease, sometimes so far gone that I had to turn away. But they had stores and shops and carried on a very normal life among themselves.

A man walked out in the street to intercept me and in cultured tones said he was Mr. Jones of St. Paul, Minnesota. He offered his hand and I gulped hard. I didn't want to offend him by not shaking hands, but I didn't want to get too close to any lepers either, and this poor American who had been in the colony fifteen or twenty years really had the disease. Reluctantly, I reached for his hand. It was sweaty and cold and clammy, like a fish or a dead man's hand. I was glad to let go. Mr. Jones in some way had heard all about our being on the island and wished me good luck after we talked a while. Before I left him he offered to give me a battery radio that must have been a prized possession, but I refused on the assumption that a man in his condition needed the entertainment worse than I.

After handing over the compass, Dr. Wade conducted me through the 500-bed leper hospital. The characteristic clean hospital smell overhung the odor given off by the lepers and, indeed, I saw worse cases on the street coming to the hospital than I saw in bed. The attendants washed carefully with alcohol after handling any patients, but the alcohol supply was practically nil when I was there and they had reverted to plain soap. I admired their courage because I knew that I wouldn't have stayed there.

The day after my visit to the hospital, a Filipino named Standobal sidled up to me as I watched progress on the boat repairs, and whispered that he'd like me to come to his home. I followed him at a reasonable distance, burning with curiosity. As soon as I entered the house he motioned me into a side room and locked the door. Then he fished in a box beneath a bed and dug out a list of names. I looked at them and saw that they were American names, men from the 48th Materiel Squadron who had come to the Philippines with me from Savannah, Georgia.

Standobal, still maintaining the aura of secrecy, told me in hushed tones that these men were living very well with Filipinos on a group of islands in the Sulu Sea. He explained that this group had been stationed at San Jose, Mindoro, when it had fallen to the Japs in May. The men under Lt. Warren Baggett of Atlanta, Georgia, fled to the mountains with guns and ammunition and large quantities of supplies. After weeks in the hills they returned to an isolated section of the beach and secured enough boats to negotiate the trip to the Sulu Sea Haven. But some of the men became ill and when a Japanese cruiser stopped at the island, Lt. Baggett and Major Say of Cebu marshaled the sick men to the beach and voluntarily surrendered. The rest of the party was still hiding in the mountains.

When the Filipino concluded his recital, I thanked him for the information and promised that when the Americans returned to the Philippines he'd be decorated for his loyalty. Even this promise from a hunted American officer was sufficient to make him swell with pride.

The Japs had come to Culion once. They wouldn't let any leper even come near them, and they sprayed every place they walked and even themselves very thoroughly so as to preclude any danger of their catching the disease. Once each day, a patrol boat manned by watchful Japs circled the island, but they never landed. We hid each time the boat approached.

The Japs had sent a transport loaded with 1,500 bags of rice to the island, and American prisoners unloaded it while the Jap guards, afraid to step on the shore, pushed them to the limit under a broiling sun, not allowing them to rest of even have a drink of water. Some of these prisoners, I learned, were from my adopted outfit, the Fourth Marines, who fought so well on Corregidor. That rice and a couple of rifles were all the Japs had left on the island, and everyone knew that both were intended for the same purpose: to make sure that none of the lepers left the island because of hunger, or for any other purpose.

Although the governor assisted us in every way possible, he was uneasy all during our stay, and I can understand his fear. Here he was, an appointed official of a ruthless conqueror, flaunting their rules within sight of the conquerors. If the Japs had discovered us on the island, they probably would have annihilated the entire Culion colony because they would have been delighted at such an opportunity to eliminate the leper problem.

So Dr. Nolasco breathed a sigh of relief when we boarded the shipshape *Ruth-Lee* and raised our sails. By this time everyone in the colony had heard of us, and there was a large crowd at the beach to see us off, lepers on their side of the dividing line. Old Glory was flowing from the stern as we moved away from the dock and the entire assemblage gave a spontaneous cheer. It made me feel very proud, as when you hear "The Star-Spangled Banner" played at retreat with the setting sun lighting the red, white, and blue folds.

In this country I learned that Governor Nolasco was a personal friend of President Quezon, who had appointed him to care for the leper colony.

CHAPTER 11

ONCE OUT OF SIGHT of the Jap stronghold that menaced Culion I settled back comfortably at the tiller and lit one of Dr. Hanks's cigars. The Little Swede was rumbling more smoothly than ever before, and I congratulated myself on having put in at the leper colony. The motor would never have taken us within shouting distance of Australia if we hadn't obtained expert service from a mechanic who had the proper tools. And not only that, but the additional supplies—even a Jap gun that had been provided by the governor to guard the lepers—crammed the *Ruth-Lee* so that she rode low in the water.

When darkness settled over the ocean I went below to catch a few hours sleep, leaving Osborne at the tiller. I adjusted the ropes on one of the bunks so that it was level, even though the boat was keeled over on one of our endless tacking maneuvers. When we started back on the other leg of the tack, I'd have to adjust the braces and pitch of the bunk once again so that I wouldn't tumble out.

Osborne had never done any sailing and was nervous when handling the boat alone. Perhaps an hour after I ducked into the cabin I heard the wind rising and the waves slapping the hull more sharply. I got up and squeezed past the chugging motor that loomed out of the bottom of the boat. The wind had freshened and jagged gashes of lightning streaked across the sky. The clouds were moving right across our path, and after each blinding lightning flash it was so dark that I couldn't see the mast fifteen feet ahead.

I turned the tiller over to Osborne, while I scrambled over the cabin top to haul in some sail. Then I ducked into the cabin to pat the Little Swede and admonish it not to stop during the next few hours. The wind was really kicking up when I again reached the tiller, and both Osborne and I lashed ourselves to the boat. If one of the waves washed us overboard in the dark we would never see daylight again. The lashing was adopted as a regular practice at night after that.

When the rain began pelting I headed into the wind, the motor chugging valiantly and growling at the commotion caused by the weather. I had discovered earlier that in a storm the boat handled better by maintaining some sail, which acted as a stabilizer as long as we steered into the wind. It was rough going against the gusts, rain, and lightning, and the *Ruth-Lee* was taking on some water, but I figured the disturbance was local and would soon blow itself out.

My thoughts were given a rude jolt, however, when the boat reached the trough of a wave and banged resoundingly on a reef. My crew was in the cabin trying to keep the motor dry, and he was sent spinning by the crash; only the grip I held on the tiller arm kept me from a similar fate. The next wave picked the boat up and set it down with another crash that made me wince for the poor *Ruth-Lee*.

There were more bounces until at last we stuck and groaned and scraped on the coral with every movement, powerless before the whim of the wind and waves.

I had been so intent on keeping the boat from swinging broadside into the wind that I hadn't even noticed the reefs, and there was so much noise from the storm that I didn't hear the waves breaking over them.

The hull was leaking in a dozen places from the pounding on the coral, and the wind shrieked through the rigging as we shivered and shook. We couldn't sink but the *Ruth-Lee* might fall apart. Toward daybreak the storm abated, and Osborne and I, wet, cold, and dejected, clambered over the side and heaved and shoved the *Ruth-Lee* toward the beach. It was to be the first of many times that we were to go through that discouraging procedure, slashing our feet and legs every time on the slippery and jagged coral.

Once off the reef we floated in as far as we could, and when the tide ran out the boat lay on her right side like a wounded fish. The trim craft that had sailed proudly out of Culion on the preceding day was now worn and rent. I spent the day stuffing rags into holes punched by the coral, and Osborne caulked seams with apo. With night and the high tide the boat floated, and when the tide receded, Osborne and I pulled with all our might on the left side and rolled the boat to the left, leaving the right side exposed so that we could patch more holes. That took the remainder of the day, and at nightfall we were ready to feel our way gingerly through the reefs and into the open sea again.

I guess we must have foundered on coral reefs twenty times following the first serious mishap. In the daytime we could see the churning water and steer clear, but at night it was more difficult and especially in rough weather. On a clear night the shimmering light given off by the curling and churning water was a dead giveaway, so we gave those spots a wide berth.

The *Ruth-Lee* was now lumbering along and bucking the strong southwest monsoon which made sailing out of the islands at that time of year particularly difficult. Day and night, we pitched in the heavy seas, making only about twenty or thirty miles a day. The motor became temperamental again and would run one day and then lay off two. Sometimes it would run for eight hours and then rest for eighteen. You might think it had a union card. When it was operating we could make possibly four knots an hour against the prevailing winds, but using the sails we had to make long tacks and cover far more territory to get just a few miles along on our course.

On one of these long tedious tacks I reasoned that the elements were an even greater source of danger than the Japs. If the Nips took us, we would be prisoners, that was a dead certainty, but if the *Ruth-Lee* was bashed to pieces on rocks in a storm, the same fate awaited her crew. We had no life preservers, so if the boat fell apart at sea, as it showed every inclination to do, we would again be the sad victims. But I buried these thoughts and said nothing to Osborne, who was skeptical enough about the merits of sailing and my nautical skill in particular.

Our temporary repairs did not hold out against the continuing ocean swells, so with the boat leaking badly we at last sought refuge on the little island of Cabatuan where the natives helped us repair our previous repairs. We stayed there two days going through the same process of working on first one side and then the other, and then set sail once again.

Our heavily laden craft unfortunately encountered more bad weather, and we dipped tons of water. Osborne bailed continuously with a five-gallon can, and we kept plowing through the windswept and raging sea for several days until we sighted an island I guessed was Lanjoy, off the coast of Palawan. I swam ashore looking for fresh water and fruit, and stumbled into a patch of poison ivy, and contracted as serious a case as I have ever seen. The infernal stuff was just like liquid fire and having no medical remedies for it, the only thing I could do was have Osborne dash cold water over my legs and back. This helped, but when the water dried, the salt eating into the infected skin was torture. When it became unbearable I'd let out a yelp and jump overboard and hang in the cold water. The infection lasted about two weeks.

We were constantly buffeted by the southwest monsoon, so when we sighted Dumaran we sailed along the shore until we found a river emptying into the sea. We put in at the mouth, and I went ashore for water. Natives who sailed across the river intercepted me before I got back to Osborne, who was guarding the *Ruth-Lee*; in the course of our conversation about the dispersement of Jap troops in the area, one of them mentioned that an American soldier named Spaulding was hiding farther down the coast. The next morning we cruised slowly down the coastline toward the place Spaulding was supposedly hiding, but we saw no sign of any living being. Osborne and I decided that he probably was just inside the rim of the jungle, watching and cursing us as Japs. Finally, as a last resort we raised the

American flag, and turned the boat and moved back along the route.

The flag was the motivating force, because we hadn't moved a hundred yards when a tall, bronzed American walked out on the beach calling to us, and we hurriedly turned and beached the craft. Spaulding, who waded out to us, was a man of about 25, from Montana. The transport which had been carrying him was sunk about sixty miles offshore at the beginning of the war, and he alone had reached the beach and had been living there for more than six months with a native family.

I offered to take him with us, but the Montana man refused, flatly saying that we hadn't a chance to get out of the islands against the southwest monsoon. He was building a boat, in which he planned to sail for Australia in December with the favoring northeast monsoon, and he in turn invited us to wait and go with him. But Osborne and I felt that it was now or never for us, and we were confident, in spite of our setbacks, that we could sail to Australia. So after taking a letter from him to his mother and family, we sailed away, leaving him standing forlornly on the beach, shading his eyes with his hands so he could watch us out of sight.

That night, sailing by the stars, we ran on another reef and had to put in for the usual two days of repairs. However, this time we had not been pounded by a storm so the holes were not too bad. When sailing at night our little compass was illuminated by a shaded flashlight bulb, but we still depended heavily upon the stars. You can't imagine how dark it is in the Sulu Sea in the dead of night in a creaking twenty-foot boat. We never knew exactly where we were going, but we'd consult the map from Col. Wells and then head in the direction of the nearest logical landing place. All along the route the natives kept us informed of the goings and comings of the Japs, so that in most cases we were able to avoid areas or islands that were dangerous.

We had been told that there was a large garrison of Japanese and about three hundred American prisoners at Puerto Princesa, halfway south on Palawan, the same prisoners who had unloaded the rice at Culion. Knowing this, we worked our way in close to shore, staying behind the points and reefs as much as possible until we estimated four miles north of Puerto Princesa. At dusk we cut the motor that had been behaving nobly and started to sail past the danger spot.

The town was blacked out, but it was impossible to keep a fairly large community hidden from eyes accustomed to the darkness, and we could see activity along the water front as the *Ruth-Lee* drew abreast of the garrison at a maddening crawl. At any moment I expected to be challenged by a Jap patrol boat, but none approached us.

As the night wore on, the wind died and the sails flapped helplessly on the mast. Dawn found us still in full view of Puerto Princesa, so we hoisted the Jap flag and tried to look as much like a Jap fishing boat as possible. The sun was only a little ways above the horizon when two boats resembling our PT boats hurried out from shore, their bows cleaving the water in a mad rush. They were steering straight for us, and I said to myself, "Uh, oh, the jig's up!"

But the Jap boats hugged the shore and passed within waving distance. Our trick evidently had worked because they didn't even give us a second look. The red-disked flag that straggled out at our stern was hardly one that I could love, but it was certainly a help that morning. As soon as we were out of sight of the port, I kicked over the Little Swede and the *Ruth-Lee* nosed down the cost toward Brooke's Point, Palawan.

The sun was unbearably hot during the days, but at night in the little bunk in the cabin the native sheet and any other clothing we had felt comfortable. During the day, the heat from the motor, added to the heat from the sun, made the little cabin a hot box, so I spent most of the daylight hours on deck where I could catch the breeze.

One afternoon, while I was sitting on top of the cabin, thinking of a hundred things that didn't concern the war, I happened to glance back, and there, a few feet behind the *Ruth-Lee,* was an ugly man-eating shark following us at a regular distance and eyeing me as if I were a ten-course dinner. He pursued us for the rest of the day and, although neither of us would admit it, I think both Osborne and I got the shakes when we thought why the shark intuitively followed our boat.

Next morning the first thing both of us did when it was light enough was to look for the shark we had named Butch, and, sure enough, he was still there, never varying an inch from his course or distance from the boat. During the morning, we fired our pistols at him alternately, but it didn't budge him. In the afternoon we tied a knife to a bamboo pole and tried to harpoon him. That didn't work, but it helped speed time.

Finally, in desperation and exasperation, I fashioned a hook out of a piece of steel wire, baited it with a piece of dried carabao meat, and tickled Butch on the nose with it for several minutes. I was about to give up when he decided to be enticed by the measly morsel and gulped a shark-sized gulp, swallowing the hook as if it had been a choice piece of Gause leg. For the next half hour the *Ruth-Lee* alternately moved backward and sideward, or so it seemed, the shark put up such a struggle. The line we had was tough, but there wasn't much of it so he was drawn up sharp at twenty-five feet. When he tired and jerked convulsively only at second intervals, we hauled him over the rail, and he flopped down with a splash on the bottom of the boat. Then the fun began.

Butch's tail began swinging like Dempsey in his prime, and both Osborne and I went down for a count but scrambled to our feet in a hurry, both wondering if sharks could still bite out of the water. Trying to keep out of the way of the thrashing man-eater (he was about eight feet in length), I ducked into the cabin and got the knife I had taken from the Jap sentry on Bataan. We both fell on the fish and I stabbed him a half dozen times in what I thought were a fish's vital spots until his struggles ceased. We had Butch for supper that night without any qualms of conscience, knowing that he would have done the same to us, with relish.

CHAPTER 12

WE HAD A LITTLE stove on the boat made out of a 5-gallon can, and firewood was piled at the front of the cabin along with a supply of green coconuts. Osborne did the cooking and did a damn good job, considering the barren cupboard. The sun-dried meat tasted as good as an Astor meal after a day in the sun and ocean breeze. We luckily had plenty of matches safe in a handmade mahogany chest, which was stocked with our other valuables, guns, and a pad of yellow paper I obtained at Culion.

We were covering the area along the reef-strewn shore of Palawan Island by this time. The Little Swede was operating haphazardly when, one morning, we rounded a promontory and saw a Jap seaplane rocking gently at anchor. The disk on the side looked as big as a silver dollar on the night before payday. There was also a Jap motor launch tied alongside, and when the lounging soldiers spotted us they made a mad dash to start their motor. They had so little to do, I suppose, that they all wanted to be in on the kill, like the volunteer firemen in a small town. With their eager shouts ringing in my ears, I dashed toward the diesel engine, praying it would start. I turned it over once.

Twice! And on the third try it gave voice, and I felt our little boat gaining momentum.

When I was sure that the Little Swede would keep running, I went back to the tiller. Osborne was unlimbering our two old fowling pieces. The Japs were having difficulty starting their launch, and when they saw that we were moving away, those who weren't bent over the engine began firing at us with rifles. When we made another point and passed out of sight, they were still firing wildly, cursing and trying to start their boat, but we took no chances on the disposition of the Jap motor and immediately started zigzagging in among the small scattered islands. In a quiet lagoon we hid the boat under the over-hanging branches and waited anxiously for nightfall. We heard the Jap launch poring over the vicinity where we had last been seen. They were moving fast so as to cover as much territory as possible, but they never did pass us; when night came we were able to slip away under sail.

About the first of September, we reached what had been Brooke's Point. Now, only a few deserted buildings stood; the rest had been leveled by fire and the villagers had fled into the mountains. The Japs had been there, of course. We passed many similar deserted towns and villages on the islands, a touching tribute to the Jap thoroughness.

An American, a Mr. Edwards, was living in the vicinity according to reports we had been given, so we inquired of the first natives we saw. The people in this south Philippines area, by the way, were of the Moro clan, and they spoke an entirely different dialect so that we carried on most of our conversation in sign language. But the men, clad in wraparound skirts, were quick to grasp our purpose in landing, and they conducted us to their nearby village where there was a better-educated Filipino who spoke Spanish.

He told us that Mr. Edwards, a large landholder, lived back in the mountains, and he dispatched a runner to carry the news of our arrival. While awaiting action on the Edwards front, we began making some minor repairs to the boat with curious natives bringing their families to watch us. They were liberal with the food stores that remained to them, and we had a couple of good meals.

Two days later, a young American interrupted us at the boat and introduced himself as Al Edwards. He said his father was ill with the fever, but that he had come to see what he could do for the Americans. We explained that we needed foodstuffs badly and that the Little Swede needed adjustments and repairs. Edwards very softly said he thought those things could be taken care of, and from his tone and manner I had the feeling that they would be.

I had nursed the old diesel along as best I could, but we had no spare parts and, if anything had broken, it would have been just too bad. Al looked at it, dropped a remark that he had studied engineering at the University of Chicago, and then went to work on the Little Swede in the manner of a man who knows what he's doing. He ordered a carabao to haul our boat out on the beach so that we could patch up the bottom, and even assigned a man to help us. A Filipino soldier named Limento, who hung around watching, became very friendly, and gave us stocks of information about the Japanese strength and habits in the area. The Japs at this time were very methodical and would make their trips of investigation about the same time every week. We had just missed one patrol when we arrived at Brooke's Point.

As was the case on every other island, news of our landing spread rapidly, and on the fifth day I almost fell over the rail of the high and dry *Ruth-Lee* when six lean and leathery Americans trooped out of the jungle and casually said, "Hi!" One of the men was the Marine who had first met me when I swam ashore at Corregidor, and he looked about the same now, with a heavy beard and dirty clothes. I was flabbergasted.

My mouth fell open when I tried to talk, but the men laughed, enjoying the commotion they had caused, and said that they were three Marines and three sailors who had been among the captured at Bataan and Corregidor. They had escaped from the Jap prison camp at Puerto Princesa a week ago. We stopped work and all sat down to eat together, and then the Marine who had escorted me to the Corregidor hospital answered my question about what he'd been doing up to this time.

"The Japs kept us on Corregidor for about ten days after May 6th," he began, leaning back and clasping one knee with his hands, "making us load scrap iron on the Jap freighters. Then they piled us into transports and moved us across the bay to Paranaque where we were dumped on the beach from barges. It was a sweltering day, the tropical sun just broiling down on us, but they pushed and shoved us into the semblance of a column and we began walking toward Manila. For ten miles we walked, right down Dewey Boulevard to Bilibid Prison where we spent the next several days. The Japs were immensely pleased at themselves for making us march through the city instead of carting us to the prison in boats, as they could have done.

"They expected the Manila people to cheer and welcome the conquerors and their captives, but I didn't hear a cheer anywhere along the route. In fact, it was more like a funeral march with the Jap guards barking out orders and molesting the hungry, tired, and beaten men to show that they were masters of the situation. Scores of men, many of whom were sick with fever, dropped out of the line and were kicked into the gutter by the Japs and left to be picked up later. Filipinos would dart out of their homes to bring water, cigarettes, and food to these needy men, but the Nips would fire at them, or in their direction anyway, and frighten them away. If anyone so much as turned to look back, he was kicked and slapped and talking was punishable by death, and the Japs meant it.

"The only Americans left on Corregidor were the doctors, nurses, and medical corpsmen who were trying to care for the thousands of sick and wounded in the hospitals. The day the Japs took over the island, three Americans and one Filipino nurse waded into the sea together. I saw them, but I wasn't thinking well and believed they were going to try and swim to safety. Instead, they drowned themselves rather than endure the ravishes of the barbarous Japs."

When the Marine spoke those last few words you could have heard a pin drop in our little company, and I'm sure that each man renewed his vows to come back some day and avenge the cruelties that had been imposed by the Japs. I thought, too, of my refusal to help Millie Dalton and her friend escape, and I wondered what had happened to them.

From the Bilibid prison, the Marine went on, the captured were entrained to San Fernando, about 40 miles north of Manila, and then carted by truck to Cabanatuan and Tarlac, where they were concentrated in the jungles and lived in lean-tos they constructed themselves. After a couple of months the Jap prison system became better organized, and men were dispatched on work details, rebuilding the bridges and roads they had helped blow up a short time ago.

What American doctors there were in the camps cared for the prisoners, but there were few medical supplies, and Filipinos and Americans died by the scores from tropical diseases, which were the direct result of abominable sanitation and lack of proper food and water. The tropical diseases are horribly contagious, and once started they spread like prairie fire through the crowded camps. To combat the disease problem the Japs broke up the large concentrations of prisoners into smaller detachments, and from Cabantuan a group, including the three sailors and the three Marines, were sent to Puerto Princesa to construct military installations.

After being in the camp only one day, the six, who had pooled their physical resources on the boat trip, waited until the lights were out, and then they just walked—or ran—out of the camp, hotly pursued by shouting and shooting Jap guards. When they reached heavy jungle they were safe, and after a few days of walking they stumbled into Mr. Edwards's plantation, and he in turn directed them to us after feeding and outfitting them as best he could. The men had also obtained a complete list of the prisoners on the island and had brought scores of letters from the men who knew they were planning an escape.

We gave the men two rifles we had added to our arsenal from natives along the route, and they planned to return to the camp that night and wait for dark the next day, and then raise hell with the rifles, shooting at every Jap they could see and running around and hollering like the American Indians of old. They were certain that they could so disrupt the camp that the prisoners could jump the few guards and escape in droves. Osborne and I left, however, before we learned the results of their plan.

Also at Brooke's Point was Miss Nancy Howland, a Methodist missionary from Indiana, who had escaped from Puerto Princesa just ahead of the Japs with the help of a few of her Moro students. She was then living with the family of one of her pupils, and gave us a box camera and eight rolls of film on which we took many pictures of military importance on the trip out through the Dutch East Indies. She was a courageous woman of great devotion. I'll never forget the chocolate cake and corn muffins she brought down to our boat about an hour before we were to sail.

The day before we left Brooke's Point the son of our Filipino helper, Limenta, died of a tropical disease and his wife was seriously ill. So, in return for his kindness and help we gave him some of our precious stock of quinine and aspirin. Since the Filipinos had taken to the mountains to escape the Japs, sanitary conditions, of course, were bad and many were dying from fever, beriberi, dysentery, and other diseases. The Japs had confiscated all available medical supplies, and there were no doctors or pharmacists. The people were going back hundreds of years to remedies their uncivilized forebears had employed to restore health, but, unfortunately, modern methods proved more efficacious.

When we were about ready to hoist sail I offered to take one of the three remaining Americans with us. We explained that we'd like to take them all, but the boat couldn't carry more and that the additional passenger—or crew member—would have to make himself comfortable on the deck. With typical American spirit, all three of them refused, saying they'd wait for the other three to return. "We've stuck together through so much that we'll stick together till the end," one said.

The *Ruth-Lee* rode low in the water, well-stocked again, just waiting for us to guide her on another leg of the journey. The motor started with very little prompting, our sails were strong, and although the bottom was patched with tin and anything else that was handy, I was sure that it would hold out. Low patches of gray clouds were scudding across the sky as I hoisted the mainsail, disregarding the advice of Limenta and other Filipinos who shook their heads and muttered, "Storm! Better wait."

I knew, however, that the Japs were expected the next day on their weekly tour of inspection, so it was imperative that we clear out of Brooke's Point before the next dawn. I smiled back at them, and said it was only a local condition and would be no worse than dozens of other storms we'd weathered thus far. So we left the harbor after saying our farewells and then waving good-bye to our friends who were on the beach to watch us out of sight. I got out our map and charted a course for Bugsuk Island where a Datu lived, a tribal chieftain, of the Moros who were the Mohammedan Filipinos. The people at Brooke's Point insisted that they'd help us in every way possible.

We hadn't been on the sea more than a couple of hours, tacking with a wind blowing off the land, when I decided that we should take advantage of the breeze and run straight out to sea for North Borneo. We had plenty of supplies, and I didn't see why we couldn't cover many miles with the wind and in that way save the Little Swede and our dwindling stock of kerosene and oil.

By late afternoon the land had fallen way behind us and I apprehensively noted the slate-gray clouds that sped low across the waves and the water boiling with foam. The wind was becoming stronger with every minute, and when darkness fell early I suspected we were in a typhoon. It was the typhoon season, but I had hoped that we would not be at sea if ever one did break.

Osborne finally inquired when the waves reached heights we'd never before experienced if this wasn't more than an ordinary storm. I told him it sure was, it was a typhoon. We kept a little sail on to try and stabilize the boat, and with the Little Swede laboring valiantly we pointed into the wind.

Actually I was more frightened by that storm than at any other time since I left Manila for Bataan. Both Osborne and I tied ourselves more securely to the boat and I braced my feet and struggled hard with the tiller. Every time a wave struck, it nearly tore the handle out of my grasp. We'd rise 15 feet to the top of a wave and then drop at roller-coaster speed and with a rolling twist into the trough of the next wave. Sometimes when on the crest of a wave, the propeller would be entirely out of the water and would whine and spin with a noise that cut through the shriek of the wind.

We tied a piece of canvas over the front of the cabin but water poured into the *Ruth-Lee* as wave after wave broke over the bow. Osborne loosened his safety rope and bailed as fast as he could, throwing the water over the side from the cabin in an almost continuous stream. Every wave that slapped the boat made a sound as if the hull was a drum. There was no way I could protect myself against the flying water, and when it struck my bare skin and back it was just like a slap. I could look out of the corner of my eye and see the shadows of the huge waves towering above my shoulder, and instinctively I'd cringe. There was no letup in the wind. It blew at least 70 miles per hour steadily, and the roar and whirl of the water and wind made it virtually impossible to attract the attention of Osborne who labored with the bucket less than ten feet away.

Shortly after midnight, I sat down on the bottom of the boat, braced my feet against one side and my back against the other, and grasping the tiller anew, I tried with all my might to control the boat. We were being carried swiftly in the direction of the wind and water, and I hoped that it was south, if we ever got out of it alive. I thought, too, that, if we should ever run on a reef in this weather, the *Ruth-Lee* would be smashed in one blow. It was fortunate that we had headed out to open sea with the wind instead of being caught inshore.

All the next day the typhoon continued without a letup. We had not been able to eat but there was so much else to think about that we weren't particularly bothered at that time. Osborne was still bailing, although a little more slowly, and the Little Swede kept running miraculously. If the engine had ever quit we might just as well have quit, too.

Typhoons have a nasty habit of suddenly changing direction from which they are blowing. Sometimes in the course of a storm this happens several times, but just once was enough to dim my hopes of ever seeing Australia.

Late in the afternoon, the *Ruth-Lee* was bobbing up on the crest of one big wave only to plummet down almost perpendicularly. I was tired and bruised in a score of places from being knocked around by the tiller arm and the waves. Osborne's every move was a struggle, I knew. Suddenly there was a noticeable lull in the storm. A calmness seemed to settle over everything. I looked up at the flying clouds and cocked my head to listen. The wind had been screaming in my ears so long I wondered if I had lost my hearing. But sure enough, the wind was dying away. Osborne, too, had noticed the change and straightened up and turned his grimy face toward me hopefully.

Then straight from the left, the typhoon returned in redoubled fury. If Osborne could have heard me he'd have recognized a groan. The gale caught us broadside, and picked the *Ruth-Lee* up like a twig and bent her over till I could almost have planted both feet on the right side and stood straight up. I saw that we were going to be overturned and was about to untie myself from the boat when the sail ripped apart and disappeared downwind.

As soon as the pressure from the billowing sail was relieved we righted ourselves for a second—then the mast was snapped clean off, and it, too, disappeared into the churning water. Every few seconds another deluge hit us and the rudder would be torn out of my hand. Finally I managed to get the boat headed into the wind, but even at that, I didn't see how we could hold out. The only reassuring note was the Little Swede, which chugged away oblivious to the havoc around. My respects will always go to the Swedish engineering genius.

We entered our second night in the storm, convinced that our luck had deserted us at last. If anything, the wind seemed to grow stronger and the night was blacker. I thought we'd never again see daylight. Water! Waves! Wind! The triumvirate was going to lick us. But dawn came at last and I saw that the front of the cabin and all the coconuts and firewood we had secured on the front of the boat had been carried away. The pounding of the waves against the hull had torn out many of our patches, and the *Ruth-Lee* was leaking like a sieve. Osborne still bailed and had been doing that continuously, except when he put a little oil or kerosene in the engine. He preferred to wield a bucket rather than try and handle the boat in such wild weather. It was bail or sink, and that might soon be swim or sink.

The tiller was causing me less trouble, and for perhaps a hour I couldn't understand why it wasn't pitching and bucking as it had for the first two days. Was it broken? That was the answer. The water had slapped the rudder, breaking it off so that little more than a stick was plunged into the water at the business end of the tiller. That was the crowning blow, I thought. Now we were helpless. I crept forward on my hands and knees, sloshing through water that rushed to the front of the boat and then swirled back, slapping me full in the face as the *Ruth-Lee* took another pitch. I spread the glad tidings to my mate, tied a couple of bamboo poles together, and slid back to my post to try and control the boat with the makeshift rudder.

I was so engrossed trying to make temporary repairs and keep from being washed or blown overboard that when I finally looked up to survey the mountainous seas and plunge the bamboo rudder into the water, I believed that fatigue and hunger were playing tricks on me. A little island was dead ahead and off to our left. It was storm-swept and I could see the trees bent low by the wind, but it was an island. I shouted excitedly to Osborne, and he sneaked a look and then bailed with renewed vigor. We had been stuffing chunks of cloth into the holes that appeared in the hull, but they would stay in place for only a few minutes and then wash out. Osborne and I'd chase them in the water at the bottom of the boat and stuff them back into the holes. I made a hurried round of the holes and patches to make sure they were holding, and then I paused at the motor. The only control of the boat was with the Little Swede and I prayed that it wouldn't fail us now.

I was going to try and work around to the leeward side of the island and beach the boat to keep from being dashed to pieces in the wild crashing surf on the windward side. I wasn't too sure that the boat would hold together until we could make the maneuver, but I flailed the water with the broken tiller and poles to try and bring it around, and at the same time I gave the motor everything it would take. For a while I thought we were going to be blown past the island, but as soon as we got the slightest bit of protection from the wind by the intervening land we made better speed, and soon were out of the brunt of the typhoon. Osborne and I breathed a little more easily when we felt the boat rock more steadily underfoot. I turned it toward the beach, and the Little Swede pushed the prow into the sand. It was a happy moment for us. If we had been forced to stay in the open sea for another hour I'm convinced that our craft would have disintegrated. No sooner than we felt the sand grinding on the bottom, we both dropped in complete exhaustion and to sleep. But not before we *thanked God for our deliverance.*

We remained on the boat throughout the day, and the wind slackened a little. We worked in further with the tide, and when it receded the next morning the *Ruth-Lee* was in position for us to begin repairs. It was two more days, however, before the typhoon broke up entirely.

Natives hustled down to the beach to see the Robinson Crusoes when the storm had sufficiently abated, and they stared openmouthed at the white men who had been on the sea in a typhoon in such a tub as the *Ruth-Lee*. They gave us food, which was gobbled ravenously, offering a poor example of western civilization. Then we went to work on the boat with native help. The holes were stuffed with rags and pieces of tin tacked over them, the seams were caulked with coconut fibre and mangrove gum, and I fashioned a new rudder out of a tree with crude native tools. When we had the hull looking pretty good again I made an excursion into the jungle and picked out a likely looking mast, cut and trimmed it, and erected it on the boat, which had been pushed out into the lagoon. The mast was secured firmly just forward of the cabin, which also had been repaired, and lines ran from the top of the mast to several places on the boat to keep it erect, just like its predecessor. Before the storm the boom had been attached to the mast by means of a grommet made out of hemp, so we fashioned another and hacked out a new boom. I made a crude needle out of a piece of wire and sewed a sail out of pieces of cloth we had, plus cloth contributions from the natives. A pulley, really only a very crude contraption, was at the peak of the mast threaded with a rope so that we could haul up the sail. We even readied another jib sail to replace the one that had been lost, and were ready to put to sea again.

We learned from the natives that we had landed in the Cagayan Sulu. They told us the direction of Borneo, and replenished our supplies of rice and gave us eight bunches of bananas and many coconuts. Around September 14th, we started the Little Swede and the island we had been happy to see faded into the distance. We were Borneo bound.

CHAPTER 13

$\mathbf{B}$ANANAS AND COCONUTS WERE our diet for the next few days, although Osborne cooked rice when the weather allowed. Once in a while I'd dangle a line over the side and haul in a fish, which was eaten posthaste, sometimes raw with a little salt. They're not bad that way, if you're hungry enough. We were blessed with a favoring wind, and the motor wheezed and gave off smoke and fumes that were annoying and comforting at the same time. I was relaxing at the tiller one afternoon, watching the sun dip into the west, when I heard a horrible gurgling in the water behind.

I leaped, frightened, to my feet and a wide-eyed Osborne joined me. I figured we'd outlasted the worst the elements could send us, but the natives occasionally spoke of their friends or relatives being lost in giant whirlpools in the Sulu Sea. That knowledge didn't increase our comfort, and we dared not hazard a guess as to what was happening. The noise grew in intensity, till it was a roar, and bubbles appeared on the surface a hundred yards from our stern, and then the water boiled and rushed maddeningly. I could just see the *Ruth-Lee*, with us in it, caught in the swirls of a giant whirlpool and sucked to the ocean's depths. Scylla and Charybdis were tame compared with the visions that were conjured up in my mind.

Then, right out of the middle of the mass of white, foaming water belched the conning tower of a submarine, and we saw a huge, dripping red disk on the side. The setting sun glinted off the shiny surface, and as soon as my mind began to function I turned and shut off the engine so that our intruders wouldn't wonder how a native fishing boat happened to be motor-powered.

The decks were above water only seconds when a hatch forward of the conning tower opened, and three sailors emerged and ran toward their forward gun. This is the end, I murmured to Osborne, and prepared to go over the side. They fiddled around the gun for perhaps a minute, never once looking our way, and then reentered the hatch. The sub then picked up speed and, running on the surface, was out of sight in no time. I'm sure the Japs saw us but their cocksuredness or lack of interest, one or the other, made them careless.

Two days later we sighted land and from its extent we were sure that it was British North Borneo. Our food was diminishing and we looked for a place to land. Osborne had carried from the Philippines a pair of army binoculars. We hadn't used them much up to this time because the places we had visited were peopled by friendly natives, and advance reports had informed us of the whereabouts of the Japs in the area. Now we combed the coastline through the glasses and spotted a native village. We raised the Jap flag, and girding ourselves with our revolvers in western style, we sailed the *Ruth-Lee* boldly into the harbor where native boats crowded the beach.

Watching through the glasses, we saw some of the men on the shore point toward us and then call others for what seemed to be a consultation. Finally, all disappeared among the thatched huts that were crowded together in the open space just off the coast. When Osborne and I landed, there wasn't even a dog to greet us, and when we walked into the village there was not a soul in sight. We called out "Haloo!" and still saw nobody. We knew that the Japs had so terrorized the natives that their reputation had advanced far beyond their ability to conquer; these poor people, believing that we were about to exercise the much-feared Jap cruelties, had packed up and left for the hills within the short time it took for us to reach shore.

When we saw that we were alone in the place, we investigated several homes and helped ourselves to things we needed desperately, such as rice and sugar, and we even chased down a couple of squawking chickens that later contributed to a feast. The Japs were accustomed, however, to leave every place they touched a shambles after taking what they wanted. We didn't want to improve the Jap position in the eyes of the natives so before sailing we left a highly dictatorial note in Spanish attached to a coconut tree. It was signed "The Government of Nippon," but I don't know if any of the natives ever got up enough courage to return to the village and read it.

Our next destination was Darvel Bay, on the eastern coast of Borneo, where we had heard some English plantation owners resided. I wanted to sail right out into the sea, but Osborne insisted that the *Ruth-Lee* wouldn't stand it, that the motor might stop, and that we should follow the coastline. I realized that such a procedure would take many additional weeks but acceded to his pleas. That night, however, we ran high and dry on a reef, and Osborne and I had our first clash. In the weeks to come, when our nerves were strained to the breaking point and we were sick of looking at each other, we were to have more arguments, but when the trip was over we laughed about what seemed to us at the time to be serious difficulties, and we are today the best of friends.

My mate had an understandable resentment about taking orders from me, but he realized the only possible chance he and I had of getting out alive was to work together. Therefore, no matter how many or how fierce the arguments, the job before us always came first.

We foundered on the reef two nights and two days, and I feared again that the *Ruth-Lee* was about to fall apart. When the tide was in, we'd get over the side and push and shove and even rock the boat, hoping to jar it loose. During all this time Osborne and I spoke not a friendly word to each other, although he did everything I "suggested." When at last the boat was freed I patched up the old holes from inside the boat with new rags and we nosed straight out for Darvel Bay. From that day on we went where I thought it was best for us to go.

Our next landing in British North Borneo was disappointing. The first village that appeared before us across Darvel Bay was the motion picture counterpart of a wild and sleazy native settlement. The British plantation owners in the vicinity had been seized by the Japanese and taken away so the dark-skinned natives had quit work entirely. We had difficulty making them understand, but they ushered us to their chief who had some education.

He told us it was folly to try and escape the Japs, that they would surely catch us. That was not heartening news and when he advised Osborne and me to give ourselves up I decided that we'd stay there only as long as was necessary. The village was so poor and lax since the departure of the British that they had only meager stocks of food, and they could sell us little. There wasn't even a chicken that we could obtain in trade. The men eyed us carefully, and their manner was surly. We were unable to understand their dialect, but they were definitely talking about us, and not saying nice things.

A bright spot in the picture was four British colonial soldiers who still maintained their rifles and uniforms. When they heard we had landed they came running, and the leader saluted and indicated that they were at our service. That gave us more confidence, especially the guns, but we threw what food we could obtain and fresh water on the *Ruth-Lee* and shoved off before nightfall. I was busying myself about the boat when one of the colonial soldiers tapped me on the back and handed over a package of native cigarettes he had purchased in the crude village general store. I tried to pay him, but he refused to accept any money. These soldiers always used the native equivalent of "Yes, sir!" when talking with Osborne or me, and their loyal attitude was a tribute to the training they had received.

The *Ruth-Lee* now set out on one of the most trying legs of the journey. We were low on water and food, but we intended to sail for a sharp-nosed peninsula that jutted out hundreds of miles into the Celebes Sea at the northern terminus of Makassar Strait. We were sure we couldn't miss that landmark, although we were entering an area infested with Japs, which was the main reason we weren't anxious to make many landings. The sulky chieftain who had suggested we surrender had pointed in the general direction seaward that we were to take, and since it tallied with my reckoning, the prow was pointed and all sail set.

The sun was now becoming hotter than I had ever thought possible. During the day it was blazing white in the sky, and if you were under cover of the cabin roof and merely stuck your arm out, it was like plunging it into hot water. Thirst was our main problem, but we rationed our limited supply of water as soon as we lost sight of land and were keeping a strict budget.

Jap transports and several warships passed us, bound toward Australia. Whenever we saw a speck on the horizon we'd sneak a look through our glasses, and then haul in sail and let the boat founder as if it were a derelict. We hoped that they wouldn't veer off their course to investigate a stray and unmanned craft. Osborne and I'd lie down on the bottom of the boat for hours at a time during these ruses, afraid to even stick our heads above the gunwales because the Japs might be watching us through glasses. We were usually able to hear the sound of the big boats and so could judge their approximate position. On occasions they passed so close that we heard Jap soldiers laughing and talking on the decks. I sweated then and it wasn't entirely from the broiling heat. We were plagued, too, by flies, lice, and all manner of insects that infested the boat.

There were so many holes in the hull that I used to wonder if there weren't some termites mixed in with the rest.

The wind blew fitfully, and sometimes for days our sail flapped helplessly on the mast. When the Little Swede wasn't working we just about wallowed. I'd labor over it until it was clean as a whistle and still it wouldn't start. I'd kick it, cuss it, and walk away and maybe try again in a hour or more, and it would pick up like a charm. The Little Swede was a remarkable engine and even when it lost bolts and we bradded nut heads with a hammer to hold it together, it still ran.

Lack of food and water and the intense heat made the last few days before we hit Dutch Borneo torturous ones. The water was brackish, what there was of it, and the few mouthfuls we allowed ourselves barely moistened our lips. Both of us saw mirages of beautiful green islands and excitedly pointed them out through the shimmering heat waves that blanketed the water, but when the other couldn't see them we turned away hopelessly. All this time we continued to duck Jap ships. One night as the sun was going down, I saw the Golden Gate Bridge with San Francisco in the background just as it had looked when we left the States almost a year ago. I stood up and peered intently, afraid to say anything to Osborne. I shook my head and wondered if I were going insane.

It was impossible to tell whether we were making any headway, since we were out of sight of land, but on the 11th day a low-lying coast appeared dead ahead. It wasn't a mirage because we both saw it from a vantage point on the cabin roof. I steered the boat directly toward the black strip on the sea, and when the *Ruth-Lee* nosed in the pliable sand we leaped over the side and fell on our hands and knees, stuffing handfuls of the cool sand into our mouths. The sand felt so good against my parched and burning lips and mouth that I was content to have lain there for a week.

We hadn't been there fifteen minutes when a group of natives padded down the beach and asked us in Malayan if we were Americans. I nodded my head, wondering if we were to be scalped or welcomed. The leader of the little group spoke to the others, and then they lifted Osborne and me to their shoulders and carted us off into the jungle and up a long hill to their village. Their actions weren't savage and I realized when I saw the well-ordered streets and high type of native inhabitants that we were among friendly people. In this town all the people had bicycles and life progressed on a high plane, so much in contrast to the village we had visited just previously.

We were given food and water and the first good cigarettes we had enjoyed in a long time. I liked to smoke cigars, when I could get them, and sometimes stuffed native tobacco and even coffee beans into a smelly pipe to get a puff on the boat, but Osborne was a strict cigarette smoker and had abstained for months. Since we were so weak physically from the arduous voyage, these cigarettes affected us just like the first one I smoked in back of the high school gymnasium; we were sick to our stomachs.

We stayed with these natives for several days and they fixed our boat and stocked it as best they could, although we were still lacking matches, sugar, coffee, and several other articles. They were highly intelligent people and fully aware of the dangers they were inviting by harboring and caring for us, but their hatred of the Japs was intense, and their loyalty to the Allies sincere.

They told us that an offshore wind blew from the Celebes Islands across the Makassar Strait, so when we weighed anchor again we proceeded south expecting to intercept the long, narrow main island of the Celebes group. We were crossing the much-traveled (by the Japs) Makassar Strait and saw on different occasions warships lying helpless on the beach or submerged with their superstructure above the water, the results of the Battle of Makassar Strait.

We had lost all track of time, but by cutting notches on the gunwale we knew that four days had passed since we left Dutch Borneo and still there was no sign of the Celebes. The Little Swede was running smoothly, and we overtook a 100-foot native schooner that was becalmed in the glassy seas. The binoculars told us that it was manned by perhaps forty natives, so we hoisted the Jap flag and sailed the *Ruth-Lee* up beside it.

I stuck my pistol and knife into the belt of my trunks and pulled my hat rakishly over one eye. We laid our two rifles in plain sight on top of the cabin, and Osborne stuck his revolver into his belt. I didn't know just what we were going to do, but I intended to take command to look the situation over anyway.

The men on the boat crowded to the rail to watch us, and I shouted and motioned that I wanted to come aboard. A rattan ladder was thrown over the side, and I climbed it, threw one leg over the rail, hauled the other after it, and drawing my pistol from my belt, I swaggered up to the

man who was wearing a cap and appeared to be captain.
He and the others thought we were Japs for sure, and their
eyes bulged and their kinky black hair stood up even
straighter than usual, or so it appeared to me. In the mean-
time Osborne was ducking back into the cabin, changing
a shirt or hat and sticking his head out at various places
and hollering to make the onlookers think our boat was
crowded with men.

The captain and crew were either too scared to answer
my questions or they were too frightened. I spoke the
words "sugar," "matches," and others, showed them
money, and described the articles with my hands. They
just stared open-mouthed. Finally I decided that I wasn't
acting like a Jap and that if I didn't get tough, they'd be
likely to toss me overboard. So I slapped the captain as
hard as I could and knocked him backward several paces.
Then I turned and walked aft, the natives falling back in
deathly fright, and whenever I waved my gun they cowered
and jabbered among themselves. I was performing with the
finesse of Tyrone Power, or so I thought, and I rather
enjoyed my role as pirate.

There was rope on deck, so I tossed that overboard to
Osborne, and I looked in several deck cabins and found
clothing, matches, sugar, and pieces of cloth—all of which
went over the side to my mate, who was at least four persons in the eyes of the seamen. The natives followed me at
a respectful distance, and I growled and cursed them and
menaced them with the revolver, and they thought they
were all going to die. There was coconut oil on deck, which
we needed badly to lubricate our engine, and that landed
in the *Ruth-Lee*. When I got ready to leave I turned to the

nearest native and socked him flush on the jaw, as the Japs would do, and then I jumped back into our boat. As long as they thought we were Japs, I decided, there was no sense in letting them think anything good about us.

We encountered several other native boats along the Celebes and I was tempted to play pirate again, but there was always the danger that there would be a gun or a Jap civilian aboard, and then our goose would have been cooked. As it was, if the natives on the boat we attacked hadn't been so scared they could have overpowered us easily.

The next day we sighted the Celebes and anchored in about six fathoms of water because rocks and reefs made a landing impossible. We swam to shore with our water cans, refilled them, and returned to the boat for a good night's rest in comparative quiet. The next morning when I tried to pull up the anchor I couldn't budge it. It was impaled on some of the sharp coral, so I dove overboard and pulled myself down the 35 feet of anchor rope to free it. Although natives dive that deep with no ill effects, I thought my head was going to burst, and I returned to the surface blind with pain and blood streaming from my nose and ears. At first I thought my ear drums had been damaged, and for the next three days they ached and pained, but there were no permanent injuries.

We sailed down the long western coast of the Celebes for what seemed like weeks, every mile looking like the one before it and the endless jungles and rock-strewn beaches never changing. It was wild country. I figured out a way to gauge our speed that worked pretty well. Knowing that 5,280 feet made a mile, I'd pay out 75 feet of line dragging a buoy on the end, and then drop an object overboard and count the seconds until it reached the buoy on the end of the rope. Then a simple computation—if it took us 10 seconds to go 75 feet, it took us how long to go 5,280 feet—gave me our speed. We averaged about four knots with a good offshore wind, as promised by the natives in Dutch Borneo.

CHAPTER 14

ONE ENTRY FROM MY log about this time gave our position as:

Makassar Strait, Dutch East Indies, Lat. 0 degrees Long. 118 degrees East approximately, course south, speed 4 nautical miles per hour, distance covered in past 24 hours estimated 50 miles. Remarks: Have had favorable winds for a change, and moderate seas for past 24 hours. Estimated we crossed equator sometime today. I gave my mate, Capt. Osborne, his initiation into the great "Kingdom of Neptune," Lord Supreme of all the Seas, by shoving him into more than a thousand fathoms of blue water. He took it very sportingly and came up sputtering and laughing as I circled back to pick him up.

Osborne couldn't swim very well, which accounted for much of his timidity about the boat and the seas, but I initiated him regardless and it helped to relax us both.

The day following our initiation the Little Swede refused absolutely to function and strong head winds forced us to anchor in close to shore, but with the Japanese flag flying.

Dark-skinned people swarmed out of the bush along the beach to meet us. Almost as soon as our anchor touched the bottom they waded toward us in swarms, carrying their bows and arrows above their heads. They showed intentions of swarming aboard. Up to this time we had always been the aggressor, as far as the natives were concerned, so their action almost floored us. Osborne rushed forward to shove one back into the water, and I made a pass at another who was straddling the stern rail. He tumbled back into the water, and we hauled out our guns and in no uncertain terms explained what would happen to the next one that even touched our boat.

They stood back in the water muttering to themselves and when they retreated to the beach we walked ashore and drew pictures in the sand, trying to show them that we wanted food and water. Money meant nothing to them, but they liked some bright colored rags (Jap flags) we used to wipe the engine, so we traded those for fresh fruit and water. Fortified by these supplies we returned to the boat, and the natives went back to their village a short ways inland, where smoke drifted above the tall jungle trees.

A stream that ran through their settlement emptied into the bay a quarter of a mile away so we coaxed the *Ruth-Lee* over to the river, and Osborne took a small cake of soap and my knife, and walked upstream to bathe and shave. When he returned I took the soap, now considerably smaller, and disappeared upstream to shave also. I was sitting on a log that had fallen across the water, preparing to hop in, when the soap I was clutching in my right hand popped, out as soap so often does, and floated merrily out of sight. I was sorely disappointed because I had counted on the soap to soften my beard. Anyway, I splashed brackish water over my face and hacked away at the beard, standing waist-deep in the stream and using the water as a mirror. I didn't get a chance to wash again until I reached Australia, and by that time the grime from the engine was so deeply imbedded in my legs and arms and hands that I thought I'd never become clean.

Feeling some better following the ablutions, Osborne and I settled down on the boat for the night because a storm was still blowing and the engine refused to function. We were to stand watches because we thought the semi-hostile natives might get some ideas about the tender quality of white meat and sneak up on us in the dark.

I took the first watch and had stuffed some vile native tobacco in my pipe and settled down to think about the war, Rita, and home when I heard the beating of a tom-tom and then more drums and a bonfire glare lit the sky with sparks shooting high above the tree line. Osborne was out of his bunk in a flash and we looked toward the village where some kind of ceremony was in progress. Were they preparing for a feast? I gulped at Osborne, with my pipe clenched much too tightly in my teeth. We got our guns ready and watched. Hideous and piercing shrieks rent the air. The tom-toms beat more quickly and more weirdly, and we could see silhouettes of leaping and grating figures in the reflection of the fire. It was like something out of darkest Africa, and the madness continued until the frenzied natives fell to the ground in utter exhaustion.

I slept little that night and the drumbeat stayed with me for several days afterward, but in the morning the men returned to our boat and acted in a more friendly fashion.

They inspected the *Ruth-Lee* very carefully, feeling parts of it, looking beneath the stern, and jabbering excitedly to each other. Then it dawned on us that they were looking for the two bearded men of the preceding day, and Osborne and I laughed right out loud. But even that was a lucky break because the aborigines now thought there were four men in the boat and were decidedly more respectful.

The following day the wind subsided, and we pushed out southward again for the island of Sumatra in the Java group. By this time Capt Osborne's and my nerves were shattered from being constantly keyed up and living so close together and so poorly. We could go for days without talking to each other. When we did speak it would be "Yes" or "No," usually the latter, although we carried out our regular duties on board.

It was my idea that we should sail just out of sight of land so as to be out of range of the efficient Jap shore patrol plus Jap land forces. Then whenever we saw a ship push over the horizon it was sure to be Jap, so we'd head for shore and hug the beach until the ship passed. Osborne didn't think the boat could stand the open sea, and held out for sailing just offshore, but there was too much danger from reefs among other things. So we played the margin between land and just out of sight of land and negotiated the distance safely, just missing enemy ships in the open sea and their inshore patrols.

One night, several days after the tom-tom episode, I was lolling at the tiller daydreaming, and I heard a whoosh beneath the boat. My first thought was that we had encountered another submarine, but the *whoosh* that passed right beneath my feet came too often and too close for a submarine. Then I saw a fin cutting the water on our port side, and this time the *whoosh* was accompanied by a resounding bang on the bottom of the boat. The fish, a sailfish, was scratching himself on the poor *Ruth-Lee* and playing altogether too boisterously.

He'd shoot beneath the boat, and then arc gracefully out of the water several times as he circled the stern and approached, always from the port side. I was growing accustomed and more than a little rattled at the fish's antics when he changed his tactics and cleared the stern of the *Ruth-Lee* with a surging, twisting mighty lunge of his silvery body. When I saw what was about to take place I fell flat on the deck, expecting to have a couple hundred pounds of fresh fish land on my back. A big splash on the other side and a wave of water that landed in the boat were testimony of a successful leap, so I poked my head above the gunwale in time to see the gleaming sail maneuvering for another run.

Osborne, awakened by the doings, joined me, his eyes widening in unbelief at my explanation, and then we both ducked as the fish soared across us for the second time. He must have lifted his man-size body at least eight feet in the air to clear the five-foot width of the *Ruth-Lee*'s stern, and kept playing the game for more than an hour, each time dumping water in on us. When at last he tired and contented himself with cavorting in the propeller wake and finally disappeared, I thought that at last I'd seen everything. You fishermen beat this one.

At one place I decided that we must go ashore for water, but Osborne didn't like the looks of the natives and demurred strongly. We had our hottest argument here, but at last he went overboard with a five-gallon can under each arm and paddled to shore. The boat was anchored out a bit because of reefs. I followed just to make certain that the dusky-skinned people would be friendly, and when high tide came and I was able to work the boat in closer to land Osborne had the cans filled with water and the natives willingly helped load them on the boat. They were not very nice-looking people, I'll admit, but we went for days after that without any sign of water, and my mate agreed that we had done right to stop there.

During all our travels through the Dutch East Indies we kept a sharp lookout for any Dutchmen, because we were sure that any we found would help us. But they had all been efficiently picked up and interred. When we passed the city of Makassar we learned from natives on a fishing boat that several hundred Dutch were imprisoned outside the city, and I couldn't help but think how different this was from the Philippines where there was an American or two hiding on every island.

When we were several days past Makassar we were again overtaken by a sudden tropical storm and blown ashore on a small, rocky volcanic island near Bali. For three days the storm raged, and the volcano, as if angry at the competition offered by the storm, rambled, and thundered, reverberating throughout the day and night, throwing up great clouds of smoke from the internal fires. In the dark the flames reflected hideously from the low-lying clouds. It was a fearful place and I was glad when we could get underway again.

The next day, as we sailed between two islands of the Java group, we were able to observe a riptide. Osborne first called my attention to masses of water dancing crazily up and down for as far as the eye could see. He observed ruefully that we must pass through them. We gave the engine all the juice it could take, and I held the helm steady for the wall. Once in the maelstrom, the *Ruth-Lee* was picked up like a match entirely out of control and twisted completely around, but thrown on the other side, luckily. The action was much worse than I anticipated, and for a minute I thought that the boat was going under. If I had known more about riptides, I probably wouldn't have been so foolhardy as to sail into one with our boat; but our luck held and we got through with nothing more severe than a few more leaks and a bad scare. I noticed that on one side of the mountain of water, the sea was light green and considerably cooler than on the other where the water was deep blue and warm. It was these two masses of water coming together that produced the riptide.

The daily threat of coral reefs, which was doing much to keep our nerves on edge, was finally lessened by a Rube Goldberg contraption I rigged up. The boat boasted a bell with a clanger operated from a spring that in earlier days had signaled the enginemen to speed up, slow down, or reverse the motor. I salvaged some rope that was on board and fashioned a three-pronged grappling hook that was secured to one end. The other end of the rope was tied to the boat, but I drew up a loop so that ten feet of the rope weighted at the hook would hang straight down. A thin string stretched from the loop to the hammer on the bell and the idea was that the grappling hook would catch on the coral, drawing the looped rope taut and pulling the bell string till the bell rang. Of course, the bell string would break so that the bell wouldn't be torn off, and we wouldn't lose the hook because that rope was tied to the boat.

Osborne, who worried most about reefs, although he insisted on traveling close to shore, was skeptical about the merits of the contraption—as I was myself—but that very night while my mate was on watch, the bell rang and I fell out of my bunk. Sure enough, we were in shallow water with rocks looming all around us. The *Ruth-Lee* drew only three feet, so we anchored, and when daylight came we maneuvered safely out of danger. We used the bell warning system from that time on, and it saved us several times from running on reefs at night.

A short time previous, when we were laying up on the beach to make repairs to damage caused by reefs, I noticed that our propeller was loose on its shaft and had been held on merely by the pressure of the blades against the water. If the motor had ever stopped from the time the propeller's attaching nut broke off we would surely have been lost, but the Little Swede uncannily was operating again when it was badly needed and I discovered the break in time. I wired the propeller fast to the shaft, and from that time on I went over the side each day to examine the propeller and attach more wire if it showed any indication of coming loose.

Another annoying feature of our boat was the makeshift pulley that was continually coming loose from the mast. Whenever that happened, and it was often, either Osborne or myself had to shinny up the mast and attach it again. Osborne did it most of the time until he became too weak in the later stages of our journey. Whenever I went up, my weight made the mast bend and shiver, and I expected any second to have it crash overboard with my legs still entwined around it.

The day following our close escape among the rocks at dusk, I was lounging in the rear of the boat, gazing at two pretty islands we were about to sail between, when two Japanese warships appeared in the narrow channel from around a point. There was nothing we could do to escape detection, but fortunately, our Jap flag was flying. The ships were only seconds away, and the passage was too small to permit maneuvering, so on they came, one warship on each side and the *Ruth-Lee* in the middle—in more ways than one.

There was one thing in our favor. Both Osborne and I were as dirty as the average Jap fisherman. I was wearing my pancake hat and trunks, and Osborne had only a shirt and trunks plus a hat that carefully concealed his blond hair. The ships were making good speed, and as they drew alongside us we waved frantically at them and cheered the great, the noble, the all-conquering, and the all-powerful Nippon, but my knees were beating in six-eight time. The first boat passed on our left, and we could see the officers plainly on the bridge and the men working about the decks. They took very little notice of us, and then we turned to the other side of our boat to greet the second Jap warship. The same thing was true again. We could see the Jap officers and they could see us, but they plowed on by without even hailing us.

Osborne and I were congratulating ourselves on our strategy—after the boat steadied because the *Ruth-Lee* was nearly swamped in the wash from the two warships—when along came two larger ships followed by a Jap submarine.

I wondered if we were in the Grand Canal, but these boats were moving much more slowly, so we turned toward shore. As they approached us we saw that the larger ships were transports. We could hear the soldiers on the decks singing and see them eating rice, and once more we cheered the great, the noble, the all-conquering, and the all-powerful Nippon. The sub's conning tower was open and the officers and men were on deck. I suppose they thought that if the warships had given us an OK, then they had no business stopping us.

Now we were getting right down into the Jap battle zone where they were carrying the fight against Australia, so we made up our minds that we would see many Jap ships before our voyage ended. Some of the toughest sailing was still ahead, because we had to negotiate the Jap cordon between the Indies and Australia and cross several hundred miles of open water.

CHAPTER 15

W<small>E WERE STILL IN</small> the inter-islands passage at night-fall and the conditions we encountered were almost as bad as the typhoon. Water rushed at tremendous speed through the channel, forming huge whirlpools and rapids, and waves burst high and pounded the *Ruth-Lee*. Both Osborne and I stayed up all night trying to control the rudder as the currents played with it, wrenching it out of our hands many times. The *Ruth-Lee* was buffeted out of control during a good portion of the trip, and even though it was pitch-black we could hear the waves pounding on rocks and sometimes could even see the shadows of huge boulders. I expected any minute to hear a grinding crash which would mean that the boat was on the rocks again—and probably for good—but when morning came we were at the mouth of the channel facing open sea, and both Osborne and I shouted with relief and joy. I believe that the water was running fastest in the deepest part of the channel, and we were just lucky enough to be carried along in the current.

My mate and I were both completely exhausted from the arduous night, however, and the boat had been practically swamped with water, which we now had to bail out. It had been impossible to bail during the night because we were both needed on the tiller. The Little Swede, much of our food, and all of our matches had been thoroughly soaked, but we continued straight south toward the island of Sumba. We had a good wind behind us and made land-fall late in the afternoon, but didn't know exactly what island we were on.

A half dozen dark-skinned native boys, perhaps sixteen years old, ran up to us, but they couldn't understand any of the half-dozen dialects I shouted at them, including pig Latin. Then an idea flashed, and I knelt down on the sand and with the unholy six grouped around me, I traced the outline of Sumba. The boys shook their heads, violently and clapped their hands and I said to Osborne, "You see! We're on Sumba."

Then Osborne joined us, crablike, on the beach and traced the outline of the United States. Again the unholy six clapped their hands with delight and nodded their heads, and Osborne said to me, "You see! We're back in the States."

I decided to give it another try, and Popeye's jutting chin and ever-present pipe soon graced the sands. The native boys repeated their previous demonstrations, and Osborne and I bid them a fond adieu and returned to the *Ruth-Lee*. We were in the Timor Sea, I was sure, so we sailed eastward, and the next day at dawn we sighted a group of crude houses perhaps a quarter of a mile above a gracefully curved cove.

There were thousands of Japs in the area, we knew, so we flew the Jap flag and went right into the beach, convinced that no native would dare refuse anything to a Jap. We clambered out of the *Ruth-Lee* and sloshed up on the shore, carelessly neglecting to carry our guns because they would retard our speed. We followed the path we had seen from the boat and wound between perhaps a dozen native huts before it opened into a square. There, floating lazily in the early morning breeze from a newly erected flagpole, was a Japanese garrison flag.

I now associated sounds I had heard from the huts on our way in with the noises customarily made by soldiers arising, and I knew that we were standing in the center of a Jap garrison with soldiers quartered in the buildings all around us, just getting up. Osborne and I did an abrupt about-face and moved toward the beach, not at a run, but at the quickest quick time I had ever made. Once past the houses we broke into a run, and when we emerged on the beach, who should be standing before us but a Jap sentry with a gun on his soldier. Osborne and I grinned mechanically, showing our molars in a toothpaste smile, and we waved our hands and bowed, all the time backing toward our boat which was a little ways down the beach. I could have kicked myself for leaving the guns aboard. The Jap sentry sauntered after us, returning our smiles. I looked at Osborne and decided that if I looked half as silly we must be making an indelible impression.

We backed into the water and waded out to the *Ruth-Lee* and got aboard, still making overtures to the sentry who was leaning on his rifle watching us from the beach. I raised sail quicker than I ever had before, and the mainsail billowed out in the strong offshore breeze and the skiff quickly picked up speed. Then the Jap realized that something was amiss, and he shouted and then raise his rifle and fired a few rounds at us, but we were too far away for the best Jap marksman to hit even the sail.

This was just another example of the lack of initiative on the part of the individual Japanese soldier. Had this been an American sentry, I'm sure he would have halted us immediately or shot if we failed to stop. But lack of initiative was one thing, I must admit, that I liked about the Japanese.

We were now badly in need of food and water, especially water, since we had only a couple of gallons left and had to drink, wash, and cook with it. We could tell from the dust rising on newly built roads inland that the area was teeming with Japs, but the next day, in sheer desperation, we sailed up to another little village, this time with far less bravado. Still flying the Jap flag, we noticed lots of commotion in the streets, and when we reached the beach we discovered that every man, woman, and child had disappeared into the jungle. So Osborne and I went ashore and helped ourselves to everything we could find that would be of use, which was little since the Japs had already been here and ransacked the village.

We obtained some food and the prized water, and snared a squealing pig, which was tied to the bow of the boat when we moved out. I had a use for Joe, the name applied to the porker, and by sheer exertion of will power and mind over matter, Joe was allowed to remain aboard intact. I don't believe Joe shared our good will, however, because three days after he joined the crew he broke his bonds with super-hog strength and dove into the shark-infested waters. He had probably grown sick of the boat and had decided to end it all, but Joe was to do more in this life than grease a skillet, so I dove in after him, and the pig was retied, squealing, to the bow.

The natives on the islands we were covering were Mohammedan, and believed that the pig carried the spirit of the devil and that if they touched it, much less ate it, they'd wind up with a one-way ticket to hell. Whenever we ran short of supplies and located a village without Jap soldiers, we'd sail into the harbor, give Joe a few well-placed kicks, and his squeals at the pitch and tone only a pig can reach would ring out valiantly. Then we would go ashore, assured of absolute privacy. At the first squeal the natives would drop whatever they had been doing and head for the mountains, believing that anyone who would live with a pig must be a devil from hell itself.

The Japs were thicker on these waters than buzzards around a battlefield, sparring for an opening to stab into Australia. I knew it was dangerous now to be traveling in the daylight, so we changed our tactics and sailed only at night. At dawn we'd head for a lagoon or deserted cove and anchor. We'd camouflage the boat with mangrove boughs, palms, and straw, and wait for darkness so that we could continue until dawn. One day, after we were carefully hidden, we heard the sputtering and roar of airplane motors and discovered that we were a stone's throw away from a Japanese airfield. All that day while we cowered in the boat, big bombers took off directly over our heads, probably headed toward Australia.

Moving slowly by night we finally reached the southern

coast of Timor, from which we expected to strike due south across the broad, reef-strewn Indian Ocean to the wild and isolated shores of Northern Australia. Moving cautiously in search of food and water for our trip, we stumbled into a group of friendly natives who took us to their village and gave us food and even helped us load food and water into our boat. Living in the village were Chinese, Indians, Negroes, Malayans, in fact, the most cosmopolitan population we'd encountered in our travels. The Chinese helped us repair our sails and the whole group did everything possible to make sure that we could write a successful finish in our log. I took stock of the supplies we had and wasn't too enthusiastic. Kerosene for the motor was gone as was lubricating oil, forcing us to use coconut oil for both fuel and lubricant. They were the two most important items. Without them we would be lost.

The natives in this neighborhood couldn't raise rice because it was such dry country, but they shared their corn with us and contributed a few raw coconuts and a handful of raw sugar. One of the men, a Malayan, could speak a little English and was the go-between for us. An aged, wizened little man came up to us before we sailed, and through the interpreter explained that many years ago, when he was a boy, Captain Bligh and his seventeen loyal men had washed ashore near where we landed after being cast adrift by the mutineers of the *Bounty*.

When the island had bobbed a few times on the crest of the sea a long ways behind us and then disappeared, I turned in the direction of Australia, a mere 600 miles away, and wondered if I'd ever see land again. There were shoals and low-lying islands about halfway along our route, and it was toward these that the *Ruth-Lee* was pointed. But there were few provisions, little water, and the boat itself was little better than a patched-up sieve. Besides this, we had lost the covering protection of the land and were out in the wide, open spaces where we hadn't a chance in the world to hide.

The first day was uneventful, and both Osborne and I were occupied with our thoughts, saying little to each other. Shortly after dawn the next morning, I heard a buzzing that could only mean airplanes, quite a few of them. Osborne and I roamed the sky with our eyes, and he shouted, "There they are," pointing toward the south. A formation of maybe a dozen big planes, bombers, was going to fly right over us and very low, perhaps 2,000 feet. My heart beat faster. Were they American planes on their way to blast Jap installations?

When they hedgehopped over us, the blazing red circle was plainly visible; the planes must have been on their way back to bases after bombing our forces in Australia. We could see the crew members and knew that we in turn had been seen and our position radioed—in all probability—to Jap prowler vessels. As a precautionary measure the *Ruth-Lee* began a series of zigzagging maneuvers that eased our minds even if it did little to throw the Japs off our trail.

About dusk a sleek ship that must have been a Jap destroyer appeared about twenty miles away. It was bearing directly toward us off our starboard bow, but we hadn't been seen, I was certain. Darkness came on fast as in the case in the tropics; I hauled in sail and cut off the motor, and the *Ruth-Lee* wallowed in the billowing waves while we waited and listened.

Lights flashed like big stars in the sky to our left, and soon we heard an engine buzz, and scout planes appeared in the vicinity combing the waves with the powerful searchlights imbedded in the wings. They flew low over the water methodically swinging from side to side off their straight course, hoping to discover us. I sat in the stern and watched. There were two planes, and they were coming nearer all the time. The white fingers of light danced across the waves, and at the far end of the square they were covering the planes wheeled, and I wouldn't have given ten cents for our chances of escaping detection. The light looked fantastic coming out of the sky and sending a beam down to the water, when the plane was so far away that its motor was inaudible. The lights accentuated the darkness, but the closer the weaving Jap machine and light came to us the less secure I felt. A half mile away the pilot began a swinging arc that took his plane and accusing light just around the *Ruth-Lee*. Osborne and I followed the course of the plane, forgetting almost to breathe as if that might help us ease the plane out of our path. After he had gone past, the two planes joined and crisscrossed the area again and finally disappeared in the direction we had seen the ship.

If we stayed where we were we would surely be discovered in the morning, yet our sail wouldn't move us very far, and it might be dangerous to start the motor with the Japs lying by so close. I thought of the pictures we had taken on the way through the Indies and of the log and notes I had been keeping. Besides that, we were in civilian clothes and would have a difficult job convincing the Japs that we were not spies. I could just see Gause and Osborne dangling from a yardarm on the Jap battleship, with the Jap sailors cheering below. The rope didn't feel very comfortable, and I rubbed my neck.

The proximity of the Japs had one good effect anyway. Neither Osborne nor I felt like eating much, and we drank little of our precious supply of water. We just sat and looked into the enveloping blackness. It was like waiting for dawn and a walk down the corridor and through the little green door.

The wind freshened, but I was feeling so low I didn't notice it until I felt a few drops of rain on my back. Then there were more, and soon we were drenched by a tropical rainstorm carried over us by a strong breeze. I stood for a second with palms upraised, delighted to see a storm for a change. I wasted no time hoisting the sail, and then ducked into the cabin to see if the Little Swede would be a good boy and run. Truthfully, I couldn't have blamed the engine if it had absolutely refused to turn over. The makeshift gasket put on at Culion had almost burned off and the parts were held together at this stage by wire, but I gave the crank a prayerful whirl and the diesel started.

We ran before the wind, and at daylight were delighted to see that visibility was only about 300 feet with the rain still falling in sheets. We were headed generally southward but any place away from the Japs was satisfactory to me. That afternoon the storm died away as quickly as it had appeared, and I felt reasonably sure that we had evaded the Japs. We sailed all that night and the next day without sighting a ship or plane again, and I figured we must be in allied waters at last. We would soon be picked up by an allied plane or boat, I said to myself, and so I hauled down the Jap flag and replaced it with the Stars and Stripes. That was almost a fatal move.

The Jap tenacity in a search was at times surprising. About four o'clock, the sound of a lone plane engine could be heard, and I scanned the skies toward the west, hoping that it might be an American ship. Instead, the plane caromed down at the *Ruth-Lee* out of the sun and, as I was deciding whether or not it was Jap, I saw spurts of flame from each wing, and bullets whipped through the boat.

The sail and rigging had been riddled but as the plane zoomed across us no more than 100 feet off the water, I hauled in the American flag and replaced the red-disked banner, hoping like a schoolboy that the Jap pilot might be fooled. By the time I changed flags the plane was in a turn and preparing to swoop down on us once more. Osborne and I stood up in the boat feeling sure that the Jap had been given a good description of us, yet hoping that our Jap flag would make him change his mind—if he hadn't already seen the Stars and Stripes. A machine-gun slug probably wouldn't feel very good, but, as the plane bore down on us, Osborne and I waved and pointed at the Nip flag, pretending that we had nothing to fear.

On and on the plane came, diving directly at us. I felt like jumping overboard, but remained standing, my knees moving almost as much as my motioning hand. Then from 300 feet out the pilot let go a burst from his wing guns and a 20mm cannon and a bullet that zinged so close to my ear grazed Osborne in the shoulder. It wasn't serious, however, and a host of more damaging bullets thudded into the wood as the Jap raked us from stern to bow.

An incendiary had punctured our fuel oil cans, and heavy black smoke and ugly red flames licked out from the cabin. Bullet holes in the bottom of the boat let water spurt into the *Ruth-Lee* from a dozen places, and we began settling rapidly. Osborne clapped a handkerchief to his injured shoulder, and I took a pail and threw bucket after bucket of water on the flames. The boat was sinking so fast that the source of the fire was soon submerged, and in a few more minutes had drenched the tinderlike woodwork so that nothing but a smudge remained. The plane had circled us once, and seeing us ablaze and sinking fast, he left for his mother ship.

The *Ruth-Lee* seemed to sink just so far and then to stop. I took a pole we had been using for fishing and hacked off a few plugs with my knife. Osborne had taken up his bailing duties again, in spite of his wound and close escape, and was tossing out water faster than any pump. Maybe that's why we stopped sinking. Holding a fistful of the plugs in one hand and my knife in the other, I jumped over the side and found one of the bullet holes in the hull, and stuck the pointed end of the wood in the opening. Then I rammed it secure as I could from underneath the water with a few blows from the handle of my knife and shot back to the surface for air.

In this way I plugged more than a dozen holes during the next fifteen minutes, until Osborne's bailing began to empty the boat of water. I climbed back in, and we both bent over cans and made the water fly. When it was low enough I plugged the remaining holes with pieces of cloth, and my mate and I sat down to rest and console ourselves, feeling fairly confident that the Japs had marked us off of their books, a "mission completed."

CHAPTER 16

WE HAD LOST SEVERAL cans of coconut oil in the fire, precious coconut oil, and our water supply had been tainted by the saltwater that filled the boat. There remained only three green coconuts that had milk. The Little Swede was thoroughly soaked, and I wondered if it would ever again run. I dressed Osborne's wound in the dark, and although his arm was stiff the next day, it was nothing to be overly concerned about unless infection set in.

Beginning at daybreak I started tinkering with the engine. It was in tough shape. Bolts bent over, wire where nuts should be, parts worn or burned off—it had served us so well so many times I hated to try and start it again, but we were lying almost becalmed a couple hundred miles off the Australian shore with the equatorial sun blazing down on us and "water, water everywhere but not a drop to drink." I twisted the Little Swede's starting crank once, twice, and on the third time it spit a few times and burst into life. I don't think I would have tried a fourth time.

Three days later we were still at sea, plowing southward but oh, so slowly. We had been so long without water that our bodies had stopped perspiring, and our skin was stiff and cracked as the sun literally baked us. We could cook rice in saltwater, but after each portion we were invariably sick. I held my mouth open slightly to draw in cooling air, but even at that my tongue, lips, and gums felt as if they had been burned with a hot poker. We just existed in the boat, moving only when we had to. It was maddening to be so close to our goal and yet so far. I had gone through so much that I didn't think I could stand any more. Mirages once more plagued us, but on the last day our eyes became so sore and bloodshot that we could hold them open for only a few minutes at a time.

Perhaps that, plus our weakened condition, is why we didn't notice land ahead until we were within hailing distance—if we could have shouted. The coast was wild and desolate looking, but when the *Ruth-Lee* buried her prow in the sandy bottom, both Osborne and I fell over the side and crawled to the beach. I know now how Columbus must have felt when he first landed in the new world. I was almost hysterical with joy, and let the Australian sand stream through my fingers like a gold-crazed miner.

Then began a stumbling procession up and down the beach, looking for water. We both had expected that our troubles would be at an end when we reached Australia. We had expressed that thought over and over again, yet there wasn't even any water in the vicinity. At last we discovered a few mouthfuls of flat rain water collected in depressions in rocks along the beach. We just about licked them dry and then returned to the boat, sorely disappointed.

We were somewhere west of Port Darwin, I thought (we never even suspected that we might have landed on an island), so we staggered back to the boat, pushed out, and headed toward the east. Perhaps it was my condition that influenced my opinion, but I think the coastline was the most rugged and isolated I have ever seen. We went ashore every day and were able to scrape just enough water out of the rocky pools to keep us alive. Sometimes we'd see smoke and go ashore excitedly, only to discover that it was many miles inland. Sometimes, too, we saw boats and planes that could only have been Allied and, though we fired our guns and waved our flag, we were never noticed.

How the Little Swede kept running I don't know. Its oil well was bone-dry and every movement was a clank and rasp. Water sloshed about on the bottom of the boat and we had little interest in bailing. One afternoon, three days after we had sighted land, we were moving slowly along the coast, and I fished out a pencil and painfully scribbled a list of things I wanted to do as soon as we reached civilization. They included:

1. Thank God again.
2. Notify the army of my arrival.
3. Wire my wife and mother.
4. Wire Mrs. I. H. Doane, the old and feeble mother of my commanding officer on Bataan.
5. Give the army the list of prisoners and escaped prisoners in the Philippines.
6. Mail the letters that were given to me by people in the Philippines.
7. Notify the relatives of the boys who fought with me in the Philippines, and died.
8. Purchase clothes and shoes.

9. Take a good bath, shave, have a drink, and go to bed for a week.

On the afternoon of our sixth day of sailing east along the wild northern Australia coast we worked our way into a large bay into which a river emptied. The propeller-driven *Ruth-Lee* left a widening wake as we moved across the mirrorlike water and into the mouth of the river. I was at the helm, but both Osborne and I were too exhausted to even dangle our fingers in the clear water when we lost sight of the bay and the foliage closed in on us from the banks. Upstream, I saw a motor launch approaching, but I had been seeing so many strange things that I paid little attention. I hoped only to run into a native village sometime soon, before it was too late.

I called to Osborne who was slumped in a bunk and asked him wearily if he saw anything. He raised himself on one elbow and answered that it looked like a boat, so I knew that there definitely was something on the river. By this time the craft had drawn much closer and I saw a dozen tall, sunburned Australian soldiers, crowded into the front of the boat, observing us. If I could have shouted with relief and joy, I believe I would have done so.

Although there was no danger that they would pass us unnoticed, Osborne and I gestured wildly at the Aussies. We were so dirty and our boat was so sleazy that they must have considered us maniacs or Japs. They circled us slowly with their guns pointed menacingly in our direction, and at the same time we held our hands above our heads and turned slowly, too, facing their boat at all times. At last they drew alongside and we told them our story. It sounded fantastic, I'll admit, but they were finally convinced and gave us all the water and food and cigarettes we could stand. We went ashore to eat and the Aussies sat around and watched open-mouthed as we ate and drank again without looking up from our food or speaking. We thanked them profusely and returned to the *Ruth-Lee* with a guide they furnished us, and just after sundown in the middle of October, we reached Wyndham.

There the entire Aussie encampment turned out to greet us. They gave a big cheer as we walked up the rocky hillside to the hospital, barefoot, dirty, tired, and sick in body but soaring in spirit. These were the first friendly white troops I had seen since the fall of Corregidor in May. At times I found it hard to believe that I was actually in Australia and safe.

That night after receiving medical attention and more food and liquid, I lay on a soft bed, and my mind ran back over the journey—to Rita, Limenta, Joe, Arranzaso, the doctors and directors at Cuilon, the six sailors and Marines, Mr. Edwards, and the thousands of others who risked their lives, and probably died, that I, a lone hunted American, might live and return to my forces and homeland. It was not expert navigation or favorable winds or even courage, but by the grace of God and the Filipinos that I could sleep safely once more. I fell asleep that night, and many thereafter, saying "Mabuhay las Filipinos!" (Long live the Filipinos!)

The next morning, a plane carried us to a northern Australia air base where we were outfitted with clothes and shoes prepratory to the arrival of a plane that would take us to General MacArthur's headquarters. The shoes soon had worn huge burning blisters on my feet, so I took them off in favor of my customary barefoot mode.

I shaved before my scheduled visit to the general's office, but Osborne and I had been hastily provided with ill-fitting Aussie clothing, and since I wasn't able to wear shoes, we left the airport in a staff car on the last mile of our journey clad in the filthy duds in which we had reached Australia.

The palatial hotel where General MacArthur was quartered was bustling with activity, but everything stopped and many mouths dropped open when Osborne and I walked into the pillared lobby. I slithered across the marble floor in my bare feet. I was burned nearly black, but ecstatically happy. We were bundled into an elevator and whisked upwards. I was announced, stepped into the general's office, walked to his desk, and saluted, "Sir, Lt. Gause reports for duty from Corregidor!"

The general returned my salute, peered intently at us, slowly rose, and exclaimed, "Well, I'll be damned!"

Yes, we were indeed a strange sight.

EPILOGUE

ON OCTOBER 21, 1942, General Douglas MacArthur personally decorated my father and Captain William Lloyd Osborne with the Distinguished Service Cross. Soon thereafter, my father was promoted to captain and ordered to return to the United States and report directly to the Pentagon for debriefing. At the same time, my mother received instructions to travel to Washington, D.C., to meet my father. In Washington, my mother and father were reunited and spent several days at the Ward-Parkman Hotel, where a room had been provided for them.

My father was then given a thirty-day furlough to go back home to Jefferson, Georgia. Within ninety days of my father's return home, my mother was pregnant with me.

As far as the army was concerned, my father's direct involvement with World War II had ended. His new orders called for him to spend the duration of the war traveling throughout the southeastern United States, making personal appearances at war bond rallies, and talking about his escape. So there my father was—a decorated war hero, safe, close to home, with a pregnant young wife, under no threat of ever returning to combat—yet he was unhappy. He considered himself a soldier, not a salesman, and refused to feel comfortable in the role of hero as long as other brave young Americans kept going off to war and losing their lives. He believed he could better serve his country as a fighter pilot, doing everything in his power to help shorten the war.

During the summer of 1943, my father made a personal appeal to Army Air Corps Chief of Staff General Henry "Hap" Arnold to allow him to return to active duty. The general knew my father, understood the request was sincere, and assigned him to the 365th Fighter Group stationed at Richmond Air Base in Richmond, Virginia.

At the beginning of December, my father learned that classified orders had been issued to send the 365th overseas to England on December 14, less than two weeks hence and within a week of my mother's due date.

As soon as my father received word that my mother had begun labor, he went to his commanding officer, Colonel Lance Call, to request permission to travel to Georgia to be with my mother. Officially, since orders already existed to send the 365th Fighter Group overseas, Colonel Call could not grant such a request. But unofficially, under threat of court-martial to both himself and to my father, the colonel allowed my father to slip away from Richmond Air Base to visit my mother.

I was born on December 7, 1943, ironically the second anniversary of the bombing of Pearl Harbor, but I remained nameless because my mother refused to name me until my father arrived. Traveling by train, it took him two days to reach Jefferson. Upon his arrival on December 9, he convinced my mother to name me Lance in honor of the commanding officer who "allowed" him to make the trip.

That was the only time my father and I were ever together. He picked me up and held me in his arms until a nurse came in a short while later and carried me back to the nursery. Left by themselves, my mother and father said their good-byes—my mother sending him off to war with hugs, kisses, and the urging to fly his required number of sorties as quickly as possible and get back home once and for all.

Upon reaching Fort Kilmer in New Jersey, the embarkation point, my father learned that he had been promoted to major on the day of my birth. Three days later he boarded a train bound for New York, and from there the *Queen Elizabeth*, and steamed off for Europe. After a brief stopover in Scotland, he landed at Halstead-Essex in England on December 23, then traveled to Gosfield in Braintree, England, where he was stationed.

During January and February of 1944, my father flew five daylight bomber-escort missions over Germany in a P-47 Thunderbolt fighter plane, for which he was awarded the Air Medal. On March 6, 1944, the 365th Fighter Group was given a new assignment, to begin training for dive-bombing tactics, and was transferred to the airfield at Beaulieu Hants, near the southern coast of England.

Although the information remained classified from my father and the rest of the group, the Allied Forces were making clandestine preparations for D-Day. Part of those preparations called for the modification of the P-47 Thunderbolt so that it could be used as a low-altitude fighter with dive-bombing capabilities. In order to make that transition, the wings and flaps of the P-47 had to be modified and tested, which was where my father entered the picture—he volunteered to be a test pilot.

On March 9, 1944, my father was the first pilot to take the modified P-47 aloft. From an altitude of 30,000 feet, he began a vertical dive from which he never pulled out. His plane crashed headfirst into the countryside south of London, near the Isle of Wight. No cause was ever attributed to my father's fatal crash. Since the modified P-47s were eventually proven satisfactory and were, in fact, used successfully on D-Day, it was generally assumed that my father had blacked out during the dive and never regained consciousness.

His remains were buried in the American Cambridge Military Cemetery and have remained there ever since. Over the years, there was talk from time to time of having his remains disinterred and returned to the United States, but it never happened, nor will it ever happen. I believe that my father would prefer being buried in a military cemetery, next to other brave fellow comrades who fought with him and died with him, rather than in a rural civilian cemetery back home in Georgia.

UPON REACHING THE AGE OF UNDERSTANDING, I began to read between the lines of my father's journal and realized that a caring relationship may have developed between Rita Garcia and my father while he was in the Philippines. In time, I worked up enough courage to address the subject with my mother, but any thoughts I had that she would feel jealousy or bitterness were quickly dispelled.

"Damon," my mother said to me, "Rita Garcia helped your father escape and return home. If she were standing in front of me right now, I would hug her around the neck and thank her for everything she did for your father. In fact, if you were born a girl instead of a boy, your father and I had already decided that we were going to name you Rita in her honor."

As a final and lasting tribute to my father, my mother legally changed my name after his death, from Lance Gause to Damon Lance Gause.

—Damon Lance Gause, 1999

ACKNOWLEDGMENTS

My HEARTFELT THANKS GO out to my stepfather, Vernon, and to my mother, Ruth (Gause) Carter, who encouraged me to start and to finish this project. Without their love and support, this book would have never been completed.

I am very grateful to Duff and Jesycene Gause, my paternal grandparents. Their words and actions showed me how much pride they felt for their son, my father.

Thanks to Mrs. Nora Carter, my grandmother by marriage, for accepting me as one of her own grandchildren and enabling me to blend into her family harmoniously.

Thanks to my mother's parents, Alvin and Eunice Evans, for instilling so many positive values in my life, values which I have tried to uphold to this day

Thanks to my uncles Woody and Wink Gause, my father's living brothers, for their tremendous support.

Thanks to the members and their families of both the 27th Bombardment Group and the 365th Fighter-Bomber Group of World War II for supplying me with factual accounts regarding the life of the father I never knew.

Thanks to Major Richard Gordon, U.S. Army, Retired, adjutant of the Battling Bastards of Bataan, for supplying information about the Bataan Death March.

Thanks to the late General James E. Hill and to General Ronald R. Fogleman, both former United States Air Force chiefs of staff. Through their genuine interest in my father's story, they instilled confidence in me and encouraged me to reach beyond my rural Georgia upbringing and to bring my father's story to life.

Thanks to General H. Norman Schwarzkopf, U.S. Army, Retired, and Colonel David H. Hackworth, U.S. Army, Retired. Their words mean more to me and my mother than I can say.

Thanks to Herman and Helen Buffington and to their sons, Scott and Mike, owners of the local *Jackson Herald* newspaper, who did so much to make all of this happen. Words cannot express my feelings for them.

Thanks to so many friends who took their time to discuss my father's life and to share their knowledge with me. Thanks to Reba Parks for spending hours typing letters, copying, and mailing materials. Her time and efforts proved invaluable. Thanks to Howard Berk, professor at the University of Georgia, for his untiring attention to this project. His loyalty, honesty, and understanding helped keep me going.

Thanks to Hyperion and editor Will Schwalbe for showing interest in the manuscript my father wrote. I deeply appreciate the care invested in this project.

Thanks to Mary Tahan, my literary agent with Clausen, Mays, and Tahan, in New York City. Without her enthusiasm and expertise, my late father's memoirs would never have been published. Thanks to Stedman Mays and Michael Mezzo, also with Clausen, Mays, and Tahan, for their help throughout this project.

Thanks to my friend Barry Bowe, a man I have never met, for spending countless hours talking to me on the phone and for spending months conducting research on my behalf. His help in shaping my Introduction and my Epilogue to my father's story was invaluable.

Thanks to Bert Schwarz, Bert Bank, and George Kane of the 27th Bombardment Group (World War II); Colonel Ed D. Whitcomb, U.S. Air Force, Retired; Bruce C. Elliot, U.S. Navy, Retired; Richard Long, U.S. Marine Corps Historian; General Robert Sullivan, U.S. Army, Retired; Colonel Richard McFarland, U.S. Army, Retired; Peter Wainwright; members of the American Defenders of Bataan and Corregidor; Bill Barsch; and the many other people who offered so much support and encouragement to me and my mother in the publication of my late father's memoir.

Thanks to Stephen E. Ambrose who, after reading my father's manuscript, generously volunteered to write the Foreword.

My undying thanks to the veterans of our military forces for forever standing tall in their beliefs that all the peoples of the world should live beneath a cloak of liberty and freedom.

Damon L. Gause, the son of Rocky Gause, was invited by the Philippine Ambassador to the United States to speak at the dedication of the American-Philippine War memorial. A frequent speaker before veterans groups, he is a general contractor living in Georgia.

Mr. Gause cordially invites all readers to correspond with him at the following address:

Damon L. Gause
1182 Old Pendergrass Road
Jefferson, Georgia 30549
706-367-8784
e-mail: damongause@aol.com